LIFE'S
GREAT
QUESTION

DISCOVER HOW YOU CONTRIBUTE
TO THE WORLD

TOM RATH

LIFE'S GREAT QUESTION
Discover How You Contribute to the World

Published by
Silicon Guild Books

Hardcover ISBN: 978-1-939714-17-6
Ebook ISBN: 978-1-939714-18-3

Library of Congress Control Number: 2019940550
Copyright © 2020 by Tom Rath

Cover design by Salman Salwar
Interior design and production by Domini Dragoone
Author photo © Charles King

Printed in the United States of America
Distributed by Publishers Group West

First Printing 2020
10 9 8 7 6 5 4 3 2 1

*To my late grandmother, Shirley Clifton (1924-2016),
who showed me how a life of contribution lives on forever.*

CONTENTS

PART I

LIFE'S
GREAT
QUESTION

"Life's most persistent and urgent question is: What are you doing for others?"
—DR. MARTIN LUTHER KING, JR.

CHAPTER ONE

WHO YOU ARE MEETS WHAT THE WORLD NEEDS

As I held a plate of veggies in one hand and an iced tea in the other, a distant cousin cornered me. I recognized her face and knew she was a generation older, but struggled to recall her name.

"Great to see you and your family here, Tom!" She leaned in closer, knowing my wife and daughter were a few feet away, and added, "To tell you the truth, most of us didn't expect you to live this long." I wasn't quite sure how to reply.

I was already well out of my comfort zone at this family reunion, held in a hollow gymnasium near my hometown of Lincoln, Nebraska. But here I was. And while my cousin may not have made the most sensitive comment, it was honest.

When I was 16 years old, doctors told me I had a rare and catastrophic genetic mutation, one that would lead to cancers in multiple organs. Within a year, I had lost all sight in one eye to large tumors. The doctors said I would almost certainly face cancer in several other areas, from my kidneys to my spine. None of them seemed to know how long I might live, battling cancer on multiple fronts.

Eventually, I looked up the best information I could find about my life expectancy. For someone born in my generation with this mutation, it was about 40 years. The statistics suggested that spinal tumors would be the most debilitating, but kidney cancer was a more likely killer. Just as these odds implied, I have spent the past 25 years battling pancreatic cancer, adrenal tumors, kidney cancer, and several spinal tumors.

I mention this personal background for two reasons. The first is that my condition gave me a sense of urgency to make the best use of my time, which proved to be deeply meaningful and rewarding. I want to help you foster a similar sense of urgency.

None of us truly knows how much more time we have. After living more than 25 years since my diagnosis, on what some see as borrowed time, I've learned that time is *more valuable* when you can see your mortality on the horizon. Recent research found that kids who battle cancer somehow emerge *stronger* when compared to peers who have *not* faced a similar challenge. In particular, when people after the age of 12 battle cancer and survive, they are more likely to experience what scientists call post-traumatic *growth*.

Why does this occur? A review of 18 studies suggests that the prospect of death leads to greater appreciation of life, more rapid formulation of values, more thought about the meaning of life, and stronger social connections. As I have learned from experience, when you consider how short life can be, you create more meaning in the world.

Initially, I did not think I would live as long as I have. Now, I do not believe it is in anyone's best interest to live like they have forever. When you view your time as finite, you build more life into each day.

The second reason I mention my condition is that it's recently led me to a great deal of reflection and questioning about the state of work in general. I have been trying to figure out how all of us can reorient our efforts toward making the most substantive contribution possible over a lifetime. This is what I have learned thus far, as a product of extensive research and exploration: *we need a whole new way to think about our life's work.*

Our current means for summarizing a person's work are grossly inadequate. Resumes are remarkably sterile and lifeless. A typical bio is so impersonal it is devoid of what makes one unique. In the chapters that follow, I will describe a new way to look at any work you do. Think of it as moving from:

You are what you do → You are how you help

The central idea is to consider how you can use your talents to make more meaningful contributions over a lifetime. In reality, we all make a series of small efforts each day. Yet we often fail to connect our daily work with the positive influence it has on something bigger than ourselves. We need a new language to identify and describe these contributions over time.

YOUR STRENGTHS AND CONTRIBUTIONS

To help you contribute more in the future, my team and I developed a new website. This book and the accompanying Contribify website will guide you in building an ongoing portfolio of your most formative experiences and the roles you play, and in identifying where you can make your greatest contributions. This information will enable you to hone your work into something that is more successful and satisfying with each passing year.

This book and the Contribify website are designed to match who you are with what you can contribute to any effort, group, or team. Over time, I want the platform to become a place where you incorporate almost any data that will help make a better prediction about where you can find success and satisfaction. Think of it as building an ongoing strengths-based portfolio.

The key is to invest more time where your talents will yield the greatest return for others.

The foundational idea of investing in strengths is where my earliest work began. Twenty years ago, I started working with my grandfather, Don Clifton, on the first version of the StrengthsFinder assessment. In 2004, Don and I coauthored *How Full Is Your Bucket?*, a book based on the essential learnings from strengths and positive psychology. This book and subsequent books I've authored and coauthored, *StrengthsFinder 2.0* and *Strengths Based Leadership*, have helped millions of people to uncover their natural talents. In total, more than 20 million people have now taken this assessment, which is a great starting point for growth.

Whether you have used *StrengthsFinder 2.0* or other tools, chances are you have performed a self-assessment at some point in your work, life, or schooling. Essentially, we have spent a lot of time testing our talents and abilities, which is a good start. But it's time to push beyond personality and look outward to purpose. The ultimate goal of development should be more about service and less about self.

STRENGTHS ARE FOR SERVING OTHERS

*"You can't be anything you want to be, but you
can be a lot more of who you already are."*

Of all the content I have written, this is the most commonly cited passage. Yet this is an incomplete thought at best, and may even lead to a misguided focus.

To be clear: I am more confident than ever that you *cannot* be anything you want to be. What I struggle with is the part about trying to be more of who you already are. When I reflect on that advice, my concern is that it can feed into a self-focused mindset.

While your talents are nature's best building blocks, they serve the world best when your efforts are directed outward — not inward. Being "anything you want" or "more of who you already are" doesn't add value for society unless it provides something *others need*. Simply put, your strengths and efforts must be focused on specific contributions you can make to other people's lives.

However, most of us are so caught up with daily demands that we continually put off serious reflection about how to make a greater contribution to the teams, families, and communities around us. This is a consequential mistake. Tomorrow is gone in an instant, another month rolls by, and eventually you have missed years, and then decades, of opportunity to make meaningful and substantive contributions.

Knowing who you are — and who you are not — is essential. But it is only a starting point. All the talent, motivation, and hard work in the world will not be valued or remembered if it does not help another human being.

Most people agree that life is not about focusing on self-oriented or monetary ambitions. It is about what you create that improves lives. It is about investing in the development of other people. And it is about participating in efforts that will continue to grow when you are gone. In the end, you won't get to stay around forever, but your contributions will.

During a speech in Montgomery, Alabama, in 1957, a young Dr. Martin Luther King, Jr. first described "life's most persistent and urgent question" as being, "What are you doing for others?" He was just 29 years old at the time. Yet it is easy to see how, in the remaining decade of his life, Dr. King dedicated almost all of his time to answering this question. In doing so, he showed us how orienting your efforts outward creates perpetual growth for generations to come.

WE'RE WIRED TO CONTRIBUTE

Real growth is the product of following your contributions more than your passions. Simply asking "What can I contribute?" leads to a better path and result than starting with yourself. This applies far beyond the realm of careers.

A growing body of evidence suggests that the single greatest driver of both achievement and wellbeing is understanding how your daily efforts enhance the lives of others. Scientists have determined that we human beings are innately other-directed, which they refer to as being "prosocial." According to top researchers who reviewed hundreds of studies on this subject, the defining features of a meaningful life are "connecting and contributing to something beyond the self."

Knowing that we're making meaningful contributions to others' lives leads not only to improved work outcomes but also to enhanced health and wellbeing. Even small acts of generosity trigger changes in our brains that make us happier. With each prosocial act at work, energy is created that measurably benefits "the giver, the receiver, and the whole organization."

Think about that. Work can actually *improve* your health and wellbeing every day. Work can also be about doing something each day that improves your relationship with your family and friends. I believe that we all inherently know this — which makes the gap between what we're currently contributing and what we have the ability to contribute all the more frustrating.

CREATING A LIFE OF CONTRIBUTION

While I was finishing a draft of this book, a dear friend and colleague of mine passed away after a long battle with heart problems, a heart transplant, and subsequent cancer. Normally there is nothing I would have found more depressing than attending the memorial service of someone I loved and admired. But this time turned out to be different — in large part because of the way he lived his life.

A couple months before my friend Mark died, I wrote him a note detailing the profound influence he'd had on my life, career, and family. Then, a few weeks before he passed away, I had the opportunity to celebrate his 57th birthday with him and his wife, daughters, and parents.

At dinner, we all went around the table and answered questions about Mark that his wife had written on a piece of paper. This gave me the opportunity to tell him how I was a better dad to my two kids because I'd learned so much from him about family, parenting, and having fun. It meant even more to share this while Mark was at the table and his daughters could hear how much we'd all learned about parenting by watching their growth.

Later that evening, I told Mark I was sure that he had lived more in 57 years than most people would live in several lifetimes. Because of his work, millions of students had learned about their natural talents during their first year of college. Thousands of students in college and Young Life, an organization he worked with, had benefited from his teaching and mentoring more directly.

Mark lived a life of contribution — to family, community, business, schools, and his faith. So his birthday night was sad at times, but it was also deeply meaningful. One thing I learned from this experience is that we must find ways to celebrate people's lives and contributions while they are still alive. We need far more celebrations of life . . . even before people know they are dying.

A few weeks after that memorable dinner, my friend Mark Pogue passed away at home with his family. And his memorial service was something I will never forget. Literally *all* the eulogies and remarks focused on how the people speaking would continue to lead far better lives because of Mark's influence. I heard students talk about how Mark had helped them stay in college, find a major, and much more. It was a memorial service, yet all the remarks and conversations focused on how countless people were *already* leading better lives, and would continue to do so for generations into the future, because of Mark's efforts.

One thing was abundantly clear as I listened to friends, family, colleagues, and students. Mark lived a life that will just keep on growing to be far bigger than one human lifespan. This is what I believe we should all aim for: to make contributions to others' lives that will grow infinitely in our absence.

A great commonality we all share is that we have today to invest in what could outlive us. After that, there are no guarantees. As Mark taught me, every hour you devote to answering the question "What are you doing for others?" becomes something that gets to live on.

*Life is not what you get out of it . . .
it's what you put back in.*

CHAPTER TWO

WORKING FOR MORE THAN A LIVING

If I pay you to do something and you do it solely because I am paying you, that is not a partnership or relationship. It is an economic transaction.

There is simply no reason why you should have to work indefinitely for a paycheck alone. Sure, there are times when making money to get by is necessary in all our lives, but over time you must push beyond the paycheck.

When I was in my twenties and the early stages of my career, my wife's grandfather explained to me the old maxim about how "everyone works to live and no one lives to work." After he passed away, I asked my wife for more background about her grandfather's career and perspective.

She told me he worked as a civilian engineer on a military base all his life. On many mornings, he would have to stop on his way into work to vomit; he dreaded going to work each day so much that he felt nauseated by the prospect. But like most people in his generation who had lived through the Great Depression, he kept doing it every day to care and provide for the family he loved.

My learning from this is that while "working to live" may have sufficed in the early evolution of the relationship between people and organizations, it is not a sustainable way to think about work today. You deserve a job that serves your life. You deserve a life that serves a job, career, calling, or higher purpose.

Finding unique ways to contribute need not be difficult, especially once you adopt a new mindset about what work is. The process starts by changing the way you think about work; redefining the way you approach *what you do* each day. I want to challenge you to think about how your daily efforts can be far more than "just a job."

Work today is structured around a fundamentally flawed assumption: that you are doing something because you have to. And many organizations are, in fact, demonstrably bad for your health and wellbeing. A recent study that tracked people's moment-by-moment wellbeing throughout the day found that just one of 39 experiences was rated lower than time at work: being home sick in bed.

On average, work is killing people when it should be making them healthier.

This is a topic researchers have been studying intensely over the last decade. My friend Jeffrey Pfeffer, a longtime professor at Stanford, recently published an aptly titled book, *Dying for a Paycheck,* that details how workplaces are ruining people's health over time. Having studied this topic myself throughout much of my career, I am convinced that bad jobs are shortening human life expectancy. According to some research, a poor-quality job could be even more detrimental for key biomarkers of health than unemployment.

A PURPOSE BEYOND A PAYCHECK

The fundamental concept of a job needs to evolve. First, a job should not be considered the sum of the responsibilities outlined in a sterile job description. We can think of doing our job as so much more than performing the tasks we're assigned in trade for receiving a paycheck.

Jobs can be great opportunities to answer Dr. King's call of doing more for others. In place of the notion that we work primarily for pay, we need to start thinking about how we work to create improvement in other people's lives. This is what the vast majority of us would like our work to be about.

In 2017, I surveyed 1,099 people and asked them if they would rather be remembered for "the contribution you made to others/society" or "the amount of financial wealth you created." Of that group, 960 people (roughly 9 in 10) reported they would rather be remembered for their contribution. So why do so many of us think our work is mainly about making money?

Even when money and your finances are an acute priority, it literally pays to focus on the value you're bringing to others. When researchers followed a longitudinal sample of 4,660 people over nine years, they found that having a sense of purpose in the first year of the study (based on a standard assessment of purpose in life) was associated with higher levels of both income and net worth over time. What's more, even when they controlled for other variables like life satisfaction and socioeconomic status, people with a sense of purpose at work *also* had significantly higher incomes at the end of those nine years.

Purpose can (and should) accompany a paycheck. For all of these reasons, everyone deserves the opportunity to optimize the contributions they're making in their work. It's not only better for individuals, it's better for companies. Yet the current relationship between people and organizations is flat-out broken.

The problem, to a large degree, is our own wildly low expectations. We go to school and gain the skills to find jobs in the most lucrative areas, even if they don't fit who we are or what we care about. We enter these jobs with the expectation of a paycheck and not much more. It is usually only after a few years (or sometimes decades) that we start to think about whether our efforts and lives are contributing to something larger.

Instead of waiting until retirement to ask ourselves questions about how our efforts serve the world, we need to start doing this as early as possible. Life and work are as closely intertwined as a couple in a marriage or partnership. If one side feels like they are not getting enough out of the partnership, they need to remedy the situation as soon as possible, or find a new partner. You deserve a job that serves your life. The key is to make a little progress every day as you continue to hone how your efforts can serve an organization and the world.

FINDING THE SOLUTION IS *YOUR* JOB

Figuring out how you can make a greater contribution through your work has to be driven by *you*. I don't think any of us can expect someone else to do this for us. After two decades of working with organizations and leaders on this topic, I see clearly that we cannot rely on companies alone to help us maximize our contribution and improve our wellbeing.

In my best estimation, there are a lot of managers and leaders who want people to have more meaningful jobs and personal lives. However, organizations are primarily held accountable for near-term financial results. Most organizations do not (yet) have a comparable mandate to foster employee wellbeing.

Therefore it is up to each of us, individually, to rewrite our definition of work and rewire the *way* we work. You do not, however, have to figure out the way forward all alone. The mission of this book, and the online tools that accompany it, is to assist you in setting your course and identifying the specific steps you can take to make even greater contributions.

The task may sound daunting, but it's not. Reorienting your efforts to focus on contributions can start small and develop over time. Even identifying how your work can have a more positive influence on one other person will help.

CHAPTER THREE

THE PURSUIT OF PURPOSE

The idea that we should have one defined purpose is inadequate; that is a grand but impractical take on what we can expect from our work. And most discussion about purpose tends to downplay the actual value of the work people are currently doing. It almost suggests that if we really want to feel a sense of purpose in life, we have to either find a new job or look beyond work to engage in more meaningful ways to spend our time.

Don't get me wrong; devoting time outside of work to serving others is a great idea. Recent research suggests that people who do so — by volunteering in their communities, for example — have better health and wellbeing, and perform better at work. Having a clear purpose beyond paid work also has a buffering effect. If your entire identity is wound up in a job that could go away, your wellbeing is in constant jeopardy. But we can also greatly enhance our sense of meaning in the daily work we do. We should look for ways to make purposeful contributions both outside of work *and* at our jobs.

"WHAT DO YOU DO?" IS NOT ENOUGH

Over the last few years, I have learned that solely asking people what they "do" doesn't reveal much. Almost every time I ask this question, the initial response is usually nondescript. People reply, "I am an attorney," "I stay home with my kids," or "I am in commercial real estate." What I have found to be far more insightful is a brief follow-up to the standard question. Once someone tells me their functional position, I, somewhat naïvely, probe a bit deeper. I ask, "So what does that mean a typical day looks like . . . what do you spend the most time *doing*?"

This is where I get into the far more interesting and revealing parts of each person's story. I hear the attorney talking about relationships with her clients and how she enjoys arguing in a written form while working on legal briefs. I hear parents speak about quality time they spend with their kids on evenings and weekends. At times, people hesitate before responding, as they realize their average day is not as enjoyable as it should be.

A central learning I've gathered from listening to people's responses to this question over the years is that reconstructing a typical day may be a useful exercise in a range of cases. I got this idea from research methods we used early on in my career to study wellbeing. My takeaway from all of that research is: asking someone to reconstruct yesterday is a better lens into their happiness than simply asking them if they are happy overall.

If you are considering any type of job change, ask someone who has been doing that job for a long time to reconstruct a typical day. The answer can be invaluable. When you're struggling at work, try reconstructing your most recent day (or week) and looking for tasks you may be able to fine-tune in terms of where you invest time and energy. In particular, consider how the use of each hour is of additional benefit to the people you serve.

We have to do a better job of connecting practical daily actions with purpose. When asked about the first word that comes to mind after they hear the word "work," responses from 1,034 survey respondents (as displayed in the word cloud on the following page, with the largest words being the most frequent answers) tell a sobering story. Most people are not thinking about their work as being oriented to serving others.

The prominence of "money" suggests that people see work more as a necessary means to an end than as an effort steeped in meaning. Also particularly intriguing is that none of the words are about the specific contributions people make in their work, such as developing talent or helping people become healthy or providing useful information.

DAILY PURPOSES

In every job, there are opportunities to have a positive influence on the wellbeing of other people. Most of us are doing far more for others than we fully appreciate. We also have many opportunities to optimize the contributions we're making and align them with what we find most fulfilling.

As I studied how people can maximize the contributions they're making, I encountered a deeply practical challenge: *We lack a clear way to describe the kinds of contributions we are making,* and that we can make more of. We do not have a method to articulate the basic nature of contributions. There is too much emphasis on the language of job descriptions and resumes. We think in mundane, tactical terms as we describe how we manage processes and operations, engineer products, develop software, or manage people.

Instead of the sterile language of resumes, we need a language for contributions that captures the humanity of what we do — that expresses how we draw on our human talents to make contributions to *people*, not just to companies. Consider how different our appreciation of the value of a contribution is if we describe our role as energizing or teaching others rather than being a "technical project manager" or "call center support representative."

To create a more meaningful understanding of the types of contributions we can focus on in our work, my team and I examined all of the information we could find over the last few years to develop a comprehensive index. We reviewed thousands of job descriptions and functional work responsibilities. Our initial goal was to capture work that society needs and values.

Next, we created an extended list of the things people *actually do* each day that positively impact lives. (If you're interested, you can find that list on the book's website.) We also surveyed thousands of people, asking them to describe what they contribute to the world in their own words.

The second phase of this research was the development of a series of questions that asks people to prioritize how they would respond to various scenarios and describe how they want to contribute. We started by asking people questions about several topics that could be relevant to finding their optimal contributions.

Based on what we learned from this initial research, we developed a core set of contributions to describe the roles people need and value among their families, teams, and communities. Our goal was to capture a wide range of positive social contributions in as straightforward a language as possible. Rather than create an exhaustive list of every detailed contribution, our aim was to find commonalities in how people serve a greater good through their work.

We then asked several groups of business, community, and thought leaders to help us understand how these 12 contributions function in the context of effective teams.

Through this qualitative research, we learned that all teams need to do three very basic things: Create, Operate, and Relate. If a team is lacking in any one of these three major functions, it is almost impossible for the group to be effective, let alone thrive.

> *Instead of following your passion,*
> *find your greatest contribution.*

CHAPTER FOUR

PUSHING YOUR PERSONALITY

A topic of never-ending debate is the degree to which talent and personality are fixed versus developed over time. In large part because of my research on strengths, a common misconception is that my work suggests "people don't change." Let me be clear on my take: People *do change* over a lifetime. Sometimes a lot.

Even your core personality can change significantly. A lot of the earliest studies on this topic — which concluded that personalities don't change — were based on shorter-term research. However, now that scientists are finally able to connect data points from longitudinal cohort studies of the same people over many decades, it is clear to me that there is a lot more room for personality change than I would have estimated 20 years ago.

There is still a great deal of debate about the degree to which personality changes over various time periods. What's clear is that personality is relatively stable over short periods (e.g., weeks) and slightly more subject to change over mid-range periods (e.g., years), depending on what's being measured and how it is measured; and it is increasingly clear that over the course of decades, substantial changes can occur. Research has also shown that we can deliberately push the boundaries of our personality, and that doing so doesn't take all that long. A review of 207 studies found that interventions designed to change specific personality traits were associated with marked changes that took five to six months, on average, to take hold.

In short, there is no good reason to believe you're simply stuck in a role that you've come to realize doesn't suit you. There is also no good reason to hold back from pushing yourself to move into a career you think you'd find more fulfilling but worry you may not have the right personality for. I've learned this lesson regarding my own work as I've researched this book, and I have become committed to pushing myself out of my personality's comfort zone.

All the personality tests I've taken over the years, for example, have labeled me an introvert. I don't dispute them. It's absolutely true that I am not as naturally outgoing or gregarious as most people I know. But I now realize that I've also used the label as a crutch.

I've lost count of how many social events with friends, family, and colleagues I've opted out of with a little help from the voice in my head, using my so-called introversion as an excuse for missing out on what would likely have been an enjoyable time. Even when I am at events with friends or colleagues, I sit more quietly on the sideline with my comfortable introvert excuse in hand.

A few years ago, I started to read studies showing that people who *expressed* more extroversion had higher overall wellbeing. This did not surprise me, as all my research has shown that daily social interactions are the single best predictor of happiness. But what does that mean for those of us who are more introverted? Should we continue to honor that and assume it can't change? Or should we try to shift our personality a little on that continuum?

As someone who does a lot of writing, speaking, and teaching, putting myself out there more would likely be better for my career. I could arguably help or reach more people if I push myself to be more outspoken instead of reserved and cautious. Almost everyone I know in the book and publishing world has encouraged me to share more, both online and offline.

My wife and friends would appreciate it even more if I tried something other than begrudgingly going along to social events. I end up enjoying these events more than I expect to nine out of ten times. Despite my joking with friends to the contrary, you can't just outsource all relationship-building activities to your spouse.

So I am going to try to shift my personality and become a bit more extroverted. I know that won't happen overnight, but I'm confident that I can make progress, and in doing so I should be able to do more for others. Yes, trying to be someone you are not is a big mistake, but so is having a completely fixed mindset about who you are. As psychologist Scott Barry Kauffman put it, "*It's good to accept and love who you are, but it's also good to know that you can change for the better.*"

A PATH TO CONTRIBUTION

People often believe they have to make a dramatic change in their work in order to be more fulfilled, whether this means finding a new job or transitioning to a whole new career. Those may be the best options on occasion, but in most cases it's important to start by maximizing the contributions you're making *within* your current work. The truth is, most of us spend very little time thinking about how we can make the job we have into one that better suits what we have to give. Think of this as redesigning your job.

Consider how you continually work on designing the place you call home. I'm guessing you don't think your living space is absolutely perfect right now. But it is unlikely that your frustration with a color of paint in one room would ever send you running out to buy a new home right away. For most of us, the process of designing a home is ongoing, and even when we're happy with things as they currently are, we will eventually want to do some updating and refresh some rooms. When it comes to work, by contrast, we often fall into the trap of viewing it as the equivalent of a home we're just renting, which we have to take basically as-is.

There is now a body of science showing that great work is forged with effort; it does not just fall from the heavens. A friend of mine and one of the world's leading scientists on hope, Dr. Shane Lopez, put this clearly in 2015 during a conversation we had a few months before he passed away: "Great jobs are made, not found." Researchers Amy Wrzesniewski, Justin Berg, and Jane Dutton have spent over a decade studying people who have successfully made their current jobs into much more meaningful and enjoyable careers. The conclusion they've drawn from their extensive research: it *is* possible to turn the job you have into the job you want.

This team of researchers found that effective job crafting starts with creating change in three key areas: tasks, relationships, and perceptions. They discovered it is possible to shift the boundaries of your job by both eliminating and taking on more tasks, changing the scope of these tasks, or finding a different way to perform tasks. Relationships on the job, meanwhile, are the second element that is almost always within your control. You have the power to alter the depth and nature of your relationships and interactions with other people at work.

Changing your perceptions about work is the third and perhaps most fruitful area for change, in my experience. Everyone can alter the way they think about the purpose of their job, all the way from detailed tasks to longer-term goals and missions. Even people who have less control around the details of their work maintain the opportunity to shape their own opinion about why this work is important to their lives, family, customers, or broader community.

One of the most important elements of this research is that it gives each of us, as individuals, ownership for shaping the way we work and contribute. Employees across a variety of organizations and industries who think of their job as something that grows and evolves are more likely to be engaged in their work, achieve more, and report more personal resilience. Especially in a world where budgets, titles, and salaries are often difficult to change in the near term, it pays to think about your own job through a more entrepreneurial lens.

The bottom line is that tailoring a job to fit you better and allow you to contribute more is the pinnacle of freedom, control, and wellbeing. The key is to continually sharpen your awareness of how, over time, you can leverage who you are and do more for those your work serves.

GREAT CAREERS ARE NONLINEAR

Most people do not serendipitously fall into a perfect job on their first attempt. It usually takes decades of ups and downs and learnings to find a job you love that makes a difference for others. What matters more than finding a winning lottery ticket is making a little bit of forward progress right now.

This means that creating a more meaningful job does not have to be about leaving the one you have today. Even the most substantive careers follow winding paths. Careers are far less linear than the metaphorical ladder leads you to believe. When you start to see the course of your work as a marathon that winds around many bends, you realize that every bit of daily forward progress counts.

You can begin by connecting your daily efforts to the way they contribute to specific people's lives — connecting *what you do* with *who your work serves*. There are now countless examples of how connecting your work to the meaning it creates for specific people leads to better results, as well as to more enjoyment in and satisfaction from one's work.

In food service, for example, when a cook or someone preparing food can literally see the people they serve, it increases that customer's satisfaction with the meal by 10%. If the cook and customer can both see one another, satisfaction with meal quality goes up 17% and service is 13% faster. You see a similar result across other professions.

When lifeguards read stories of people's lives being saved, they are more vigilant on the job. When telephone-based fund-raisers hear from the beneficiaries of their work, they are more motivated and raise far more funds for their cause. Even when the only people you serve are internal customers or colleagues, connecting the work you do with the direct contribution it makes has tangible benefits.

In a Harvard study, field workers who harvested tomatoes watched videos of the way their contribution helped colleagues in the factory another step down the supply chain. In comparison to a control group, the workers who watched this short video experienced a 7% increase in productivity, as measured by tons of tomatoes harvested per hour. My takeaway from all this research is that people experience a far greater sense of belonging and more sustainable wellbeing when they connect their efforts in the moment with a larger influence on others.

CONNECTING YOUR CONTRIBUTIONS

On a weekly basis, I hear from people who claim to be dissatisfied or lost in their career. In most of these cases, people ask me questions about how to make their work more fulfilling once they have already started sending resumes around to prospective employers. The problem is, once that mental switch gets flipped, it's usually too late.

The time to be asking tough questions about whether you can make your current job into a sustainable worklife is as early as possible. Start with a very basic question: *Who can, does, or will eventually benefit from my efforts?* See if you can answer with the names of actual people, not abstract groups.

Even when you can (literally) see the people who benefit from your work every day, it can still be difficult to acknowledge the value you are creating and to remind yourself of the meaning behind these efforts. I hear from teachers who were in a rut until they found a way to recognize the daily influence they were having on the growth and development of at least one child. In my work with hospice nurses, who spend most of their time dealing with the very ill and dying, I have heard countless stories from nurses who got so caught up in the routine and mechanics of their job that they failed to acknowledge the meaning created in the course of their work.

A commonality I have observed, across professions, is that *your contributions come into clearest view as you get closer to the source.* The more you can learn about a person who directly benefits from your time and effort, the more motivation you will have to improve that person's life in the future. Learning as much as you can about the people you serve can also push you to leverage your talents in entirely new ways.

CHAPTER FIVE

A MAP FOR CREATING MEANING

The tools in this book and on the contribify.com website are designed to help you gain a better understanding of *who you are* — for the sake of *doing more for other people.* Extraordinary progress has been made over the last two decades on the topics of human strengths and global well-being. Yet many of us still struggle with how to apply these findings to our daily routines.

This is where I am hoping the tools that accompany this book are useful for you and for use with groups and teams. What follows is a brief description of what you will find on the website using your unique code. If you prefer to dive right into the online tools, please *use the unique code (located at the back of this book) to register and build your initial profile.*

THE CONTRIBIFY INVENTORY

The Contribify inventory is a series of questions that asks you to prioritize activities and situations that describe you or appeal to you most. This app will then show you the top three areas where you have the most potential for contribution.

It will take approximately 20 minutes to answer these questions; the results should help guide your learning throughout the chapters that follow. The inventory will essentially help you uncover the best ways to have a positive influence in the context of a team, peer group, or family.

Focus on the top three Contributions that best fit you and are what the world around you needs. As you look at your top three, keep in mind that this is where you are most likely to make meaningful contributions. Whether your contributions are aimed at serving a family, team, customer, or community, these are some of the best places to start.

What's essential over time is for your own discovery to turn into a discussion with the most important people in your work and life. Start with your spouse, one of your best friends, or a mentor. Then expand the conversation to teams, groups, and organizations — places where you can help others uncover how they can maximize their contribution to the world.

DEFINING ROLES

The inventory will also ask about the defining roles you play in work and life. The first roles that come to mind for me are those of being a dad and husband, which are also at the forefront in terms of importance. Beyond that, I also play a role and contribute as a researcher, writer, and teacher in wider communities. Think of your defining roles as something in between what you want people to see you as today and what you want to be remembered as when you are gone.

You may notice, as you think this through, how superficial markers of status like titles, wealth, and number of social connections fade away. In the end, few will care if you were a senior vice-president, had 10,000 social media followers, or had a million dollars. What *will* matter is that you were a loving friend, great developer of people, or someone who strengthened your community.

The word cloud on the following page shows some of the most common words we have heard, after taking thousands of people through this exercise. I hope they help you generate ideas.

It's critical to note how you make distinct contributions within the context of every role you play. Even within very defined roles at work, people are often a part of multiple teams that need quite different contributions. The key is for each person to have clarity about what they can (and are expected to) contribute — in any role.

provider chef entertainer mother listener
supporter negotiator consultant parent retiree
journalist manager plumber lifeline breadwinner nurse cook
salesperson engineer director spouse teacher wife boss advisor doctor
uncle sister educator husband brother scientist friend collaborator
partner grandfather medic juggler owner son example supervisor
researcher peacekeeper counselor coach leader caregiver writer father speaker
student mentor model follower attorney
daughter philanthropist organizer neighbor grandmother
mediator volunteer

MILES (MOST INFLUENTIAL LIFE EXPERIENCES)

To complete the MILES section of the inventory, go *back* and identify a few of the most formative experiences of your lifetime. What are the events, moments, or periods of time that most positively influenced who you are today?

Try to think beyond common and expected life events like graduations and weddings. Think about some of the signature stories you tell others when describing why you do what you do today. Perhaps there were a few surprises that seemed unwelcome at the time but led to a great deal of personal growth.

Start with experiences that had a decidedly positive influence on the trajectory of your work and life. Experiences that led to growth are the key. So, if there are somber or challenging experiences that produced later growth, add those in, especially if you feel comfortable sharing those stories with friends or colleagues.

See if you can identify a few signature stories that are worth sharing because they help explain who you are to others. If it helps, try going in chronological order or asking a friend who knows you well for their ideas. As you review some of your most influential life experiences, consider how they also affected the people you care about most, and those you serve through your work. This will help you to see how you can create more meaningful experiences for yourself and others in the future.

OTHER KEY ELEMENTS

These initial questions are just a starting point in building your profile. The initial inventory will also ask you for a few key descriptors of your strengths. Feel free to use labels from assessments or use your own words as you would in a conversation or a job interview.

As we learn more from others, we will add more elements to this profile. We also need to hear your ideas and examples for building on each of the 12 Contributions. As you read through Part II, please send your ideas and examples to us through the Contribify website. They will be reviewed for possible inclusion in future editions.

Contribution is the sum of
what grows when you are gone.

CHAPTER SIX

ANSWERING LIFE'S GREATEST QUESTION

You create meaning when your motivators, abilities, and purpose meet to serve the world. Knowing the first two things about yourself is important, yet that is only half of the essential supply-and-demand equation. And all of the self-awareness in the world can quickly go to waste if you fail to keep learning about what the world needs from you and how you can best serve others.

This is why the second part of this book is designed to serve as a guide and reference for contributing more over time. For each of the 12 primary Contributions, you will find a detailed description, examples of what it looks like in action, and ideas about how you can do more for others, teams, and organizations. You will also see a visual overview of how each

Contribution fits into the broader team needs of creating, operating, and relating.

Finding a way to positively influence others through your work requires ongoing analysis, similar to what companies do with their products and services. Much as an organization is unlikely to invest millions of dollars in a product that has a small chance of serving many customers, you don't want to devote thousands of hours of your learning and development time to an area for which there is little demand from your employer or community.

This is one of the critiques of the "follow your passion" advice — that it presumes you are at the center of the world, and pursuing your own joy (not service of others) is the objective. I have found that those who leave a lasting mark on the world, in contrast, are always asking *what they can give.*

Exploring specific actions to take, starting with this question, allows you to continually redirect your talents to what's needed most in the social circles close to you. Take a moment now to think about some of the most urgent and acute needs in your immediate environment. Seek out specific problems and challenges that could benefit from your time and attention.

Start asking what the world around you needs today. I know from my deeply personal experience that you *don't* have tomorrow to do what matters most. Tomorrow turns into the next day, but you always have today.

WHAT CAN I GIVE?

As you ask this question more frequently, you may notice how it helps to align your work with the meaning it creates for another person each day. This is where the future of work lies: in much more efficiently matching who you are with what the world needs. Yet getting there will always be a winding road with ups and downs.

My last challenge for you is a simple one: I want you to try to go forward with much higher expectations regarding the fundamental relationship between you and your work. Based on my experience and research, you should be able to:

▶ Do work that improves the wellbeing of people you love.
▶ Leave work healthier (or at least not worse off) than when you arrived.
▶ Work for a company with leaders who value their own wellbeing, and yours.
▶ Do your work without having to sit in a chair all day.
▶ Be treated fairly, based on merit.
▶ Have as much freedom, autonomy, and control as possible.
▶ Spend at least one hour per day doing something that gives you great energy.

Whether you are an individual contributor, manager, or leader, fixing the broken social contract between people and work starts with you. When you are able to make your work more enjoyable and purposeful, that possibility will be greater for others. The only open question is how long it will take you, the teams you are part of, and the organizations around you to get to this place where "work" is a far more meaningful and integral part of your lives.

It starts today.

PART II

THE
12
CONTRIBUTIONS

TEAM CONTRIBUTIONS

What the World Needs

OPERATE
Organizing
Achieving
Adapting
Scaling

CREATE
Initiating
Challenging
Teaching
Visioning

RELATE
Connecting
Energizing
Perceiving
Influencing

INDIVIDUAL CONTRIBUTIONS

What Are You Doing for Others?

CREATE

Initiating: *How do we get started?*
Challenging: *Are we doing the right things?*
Teaching: *What do people need to know?*
Visioning: *What should we do next?*

RELATE

Connecting: *How do we connect people to our mission?*
Energizing: *How do we get and stay charged?*
Perceiving: *What does each person need?*
Influencing: *How can we grow our client base?*

OPERATE

Organizing: *How do we make things run smoothly?*
Achieving: *How can we get more done?*
Adapting: *How can we adapt quickly to changes?*
Scaling: *How can we reach more people?*

CHAPTER SEVEN

CREATE

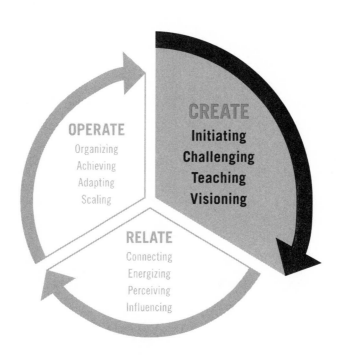

CREATE
Initiating
Challenging
Teaching
Visioning

OPERATE
Organizing
Achieving
Adapting
Scaling

RELATE
Connecting
Energizing
Perceiving
Influencing

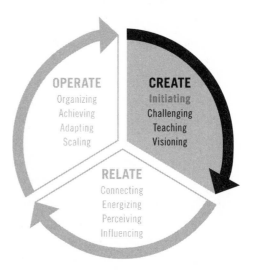

INITIATING

HOW DO WE GET STARTED?

"The secret of getting ahead is getting started."
—MARK TWAIN

nitiating new efforts between people is what makes any team or group work. If you are motivated by connecting people with one another, you are one of the most valuable hubs of any social network. This can help motivate you to initiate new conversations, share more information, and bring groups together with a common purpose.

People will look to you when they need a friend to listen. Keep asking great questions to get people talking. Plan events and conversations between people who will have common interests. If you continue to use this motivation to bring people together, countless networks will grow because of your efforts.

It is also important to remember to continually reinvest in the closest relationships you have today. While it is often easy to take these long-term ties for granted, much of your source for lifelong wellbeing lies within these friendships. Plan regular meals, trips, events, walks, or outings to ensure you stay in touch with some of the people who matter most.

Initiators often make quick decisions, act, and move on with remarkable speed. Friends and colleagues know they can be very open around people who are self-confident, in large part because they run at a constant mood throughout the day. Two common factors that slow people down, stress and regret, are not as big of an issue for those with high self-confidence, which enables them to keep moving forward.

Help others understand your internal drive so they understand you are not "brushing off" their feelings and emotions.

Be aware that many people around you are unlikely to make decisions as quickly and as free of regret as you. Tap into this confidence when you need someone to move a project or group forward at a faster pace. Note how this self-confidence is often contagious and leads to more progress throughout an entire network.

CONTRIBUTING TO TEAMS:

▶ People likely know you provide the fuel for social interaction within your friend, family, and work circles. As you go about organizing gatherings and creating conversations, try to take time to reflect on the meaning this creates for others.

▶ Consider all the groups you are a part of today. Identify one that needs even more diversity of thought, expertise, ethnicity, age, or any other perspective. Craft a plan for bringing this diversity to a team that matters.

▶ Right now, start planning in your mind two or three events that will get your family or work team out of its normal operating environment for at least a day. You can help structure more meaningful experiences for these groups.

▶ Your confidence can quickly energize a team. When groups are struggling with more challenging assignments and missions, help people see a more hopeful outcome using very specific language.

▶ Even though you are likely to maintain a consistent emotional temperature throughout the day, take time to notice and relish the small moments when your work creates meaning or makes a difference for another person.

▶ When you are working on a larger or longer-term project, help others make faster decisions to speed things up along the way. You are likely more comfortable than most people with making a call and moving on.

CONTRIBUTING TO OTHERS' LIVES:

▶ Focus even more of your daily energy on giving people your truly undivided attention. That is one thing almost everyone is lacking today: a friend who is just a world-class listener. You likely do this more naturally and enjoy it more than others.

▶ Even on days when you are busiest, take a few moments to initiate new conversations. Remember that you can never get back a day when you did not have enough social interaction to thrive.

▶ Plan one-on-one time with your best friend in the next month. This relationship likely plays an outsized role in determining your health and wellbeing; use this time as a reminder of that.

▶ Friends are more likely to let their guard down in your company. They know they don't need to worry about what they say that might offend. Keep in mind that this does not always work the other way around in terms of how candid you can be with a friend.

▶ When a friend or colleague is struggling, give them specific ideas about how they can get through those hard times without letting it bring them and others down. You have a natural ability to do this well; let others learn from you.

THE ENERGY TO BE YOUR BEST:

▶ Ask yourself this simple question on a daily basis: *How can I spend time with the right people while doing things that improve our health in parallel?*

▶ Bring groups in your social circles together for the sake of activity. Simply spending time being active with colleagues, for example, is invaluable for relationships and productivity.

▶ Talk to your friends about some of the healthiest things they do. You can be a hub for information about great ideas for integrating healthier habits into the workspace.

▶ Challenge yourself to maintain as consistent an exercise or activity schedule as possible. This will help you to maintain your high levels of stability and keep stress to a bare minimum.

▶ Spend time talking with a friend or colleague about how the food you eat influences your physical energy levels. Because friends know they can speak very freely around you, this is a great way to learn new tips and tactics.

▶ Use pre-commitment to maintain discipline about getting enough sleep, eating the right foods, and being active during the workday. Tell people what you are planning to do and share your goals. Your expectations and others' perceptions will help hold you accountable.

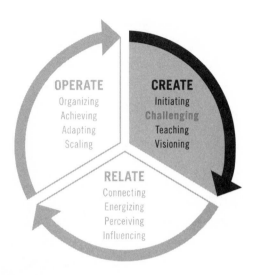

CHALLENGING

ARE WE DOING THE RIGHT THINGS?

*"The power to question is the basis
of all human progress."*
—INDIRA GANDHI

C hallenging other people and conventional wisdom is one of the most difficult things to do. If you are motivated by challenging the status quo, you have a unique opportunity to help others grow more rapidly and ensure people are focused on the right outcomes.

When groups need someone to take charge and turn around a stagnant project, you can be there to hold people accountable. You may also be motivated to push people, so instead of doing something that's merely good, they take it to a level of excellence. Use this unique knack for candor to help friends and colleagues drive forward.

You are also in a unique position to do something original. One contribution you can make to a team is to push them to do things a little bit differently to improve the end product for people you serve. When you feel you intrinsically know the right thing to do, take charge and lead the group forward.

You are likely to have an inquisitive nature, which means you are always looking for new sources of information. Even when that new information is inconsistent with what you already know or believe in, you get a thrill from the new learning itself, and even from proving yourself wrong.

One challenge that comes with being naturally curious is that you can learn, read, and ask questions almost indefinitely. Be aware that at some point, other people and groups often need to move to action. While your ideas and questions can be a great asset at the outset of any conversation or project, it is important to ensure they don't get in the way of others getting things done.

Being provocative also means you may rub people the wrong way at various points throughout the day. To you, even open disagreements can be a positive sign of growth, but be aware that conflict can lead some people to shut down. Ensure that others at least know they have been heard, even when you are challenging people to move forward at a faster pace.

While it will not always be easy for people to hear your challenging thoughts, without this type of voice in the mix, everything would stagnate. When others need a little push to get more done or advice on a topic, notice how you can move them forward. Inquisitive people keep us all moving toward a brighter and more exciting future. Groups need you to stretch their knowledge base, thinking, and imagination. See if you can notice how the people around you are more open to new experiences and more innovative because of your influence.

CONTRIBUTING TO TEAMS:

▶ One activity that motivates you more than others is pushing people to take performance to a new level. This is where much of the meaning created by work product is generated. Spend a little time every day challenging someone else to do what they might not have imagined is possible.

▶ Plan a few hours of dedicated thought to consider new activities you could make happen, and outcomes that have not been produced before. This should give you even more motivation to pursue objectives you may have been putting off for a while.

▶ To do big things, someone has to take charge and motivate people to move forward. Even if it entails challenging people or norms, embrace your natural ability to do this better than others.

▶ The thrill you derive from learning and new ideas sets you apart from others. This gives you a unique opportunity to inspire others with your creativity and help them see a brighter future.

▶ Your open-mindedness puts you in a unique position to try new new approaches, whereas others will be more resistant to change. Keep trying new things and telling others about your experiences.

▶ Keep asking questions that challenge your conventional wisdom. Even though you are likely to have a deeper awareness of your own emotional state than most people, it is important to also ask continuous questions of friends, colleagues, and family members.

▶ People pay more attention to provocative thoughts. Use your unique ability to challenge other people on a daily basis. Just remember that it is possible to challenge people through both debate and encouragement.

▶ Remember that people likely count on you to be strong when they are facing challenges. See if you can identify a few people who need to borrow some of your confidence and strength to see something through.

▶ To create any new product, service, or innovation, you need to have the right people in the right roles — the places where they can be their best. You are likely more selective and discerning than others in this regard, so make sure your advice is heard when you're assembling new teams in particular.

CONTRIBUTING TO OTHERS' LIVES:

▶ Recognize that almost everyone needs a partner at work who challenges them to do more on a weekly basis. Think of two specific people who look to you for this, and create a plan for challenging them to do more over the next year.

▶ When a project is behind schedule or struggling, many people avoid it; you, however, see it as an opportunity. Use these opportunities to rally new people and teams that have not worked together before.

- Find ways to measure and track your work for the sake of motivating yourself. Keep in mind that some colleagues may not share your competitive spirit and will need to be motivated in other ways.

- Try to spend a bit more time with people who do not share your views and may even disagree with you regularly. Even though they take more effort, these conversations challenge you to look at problems from perspectives you may not have considered.

- Almost all new ideas are the product of multiple interactions with other people. Think about the people in your social surroundings who constantly stimulate new ideas for you, and invest in frequent conversations with those individuals.

- Use your love for trying new activities to create experiences for your family, friends, and peer groups. Help the people you care about try new things they might never experience if not encouraged to do so by someone like you.

- Friends are likely to come to you for advice when they are stuck. When they do, spend time asking probing questions and listening thoroughly before giving them your feedback.

- Identify two or three friends who enjoy provocative debates with you. When engaging in this type of conversation, it's important to ensure that both people enjoy a little bit of disagreement and can tolerate the same level of conflict.

THE ENERGY TO BE YOUR BEST:

▶ You have to be the first one to take charge of your own physical health. Because you are likely a leadership example to others, think of very specific things you can do to show the social circles around you what you do every day to prove you value your physical health.

▶ Hold your friends and family members accountable, even in subtle ways, for commitments they have made to exercise more, eat better, or sleep more. You can simply ask questions about how things are going for them in these areas. Merely by showing an interest, you will let people know you are holding them accountable.

▶ Don't forget that when it comes to your own healthy choices, you may need people or systems to hold *you* accountable for your commitments. Make sure there is at least one person who regularly asks if you are getting enough activity and downtime, and doing well with your food and sleep choices.

▶ One of the best ways to stay healthy is to engage your passion for learning in the process. The more you learn about how your body reacts to specific foods and routines, the more likely you are to make better choices today.

▶ Use your natural curiosity to try as many new foods as possible in the next year. Set a goal of finding five new dishes that are composed primarily of vegetables and other healthy items.

▶ Find a few novel ways for people to be more active while they work. Challenge yourself to take one piece of your daily work routine that drains your physical energy the most, and find a creative way to make it energizing.

▶ Turn your ability to challenge toward your own approach to your physical health. Set two or three ambitious goals related to your diet or activity levels today.

▶ Engage in diet debates. There are more debates out there about what foods and drinks are good and bad for you than most people can keep track of. This actually makes for fun discussion if you invest time in learning more about this topic.

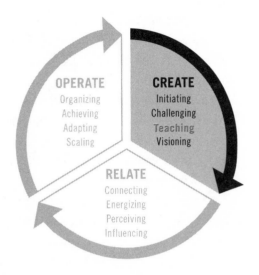

TEACHING:
WHAT DO PEOPLE NEED TO KNOW?

*"Education is the most powerful weapon which
you can use to change the world."*
—NELSON MANDELA

Without learning, it is all but impossible to grow. If learning is one of your best motivators, you can bring a great deal of information, objectivity, and creativity to group discussions. To make good decisions and find the right answers with consistency, teams need to sort through many options. This often entails studying what has worked before, accumulating information, and discovering patterns and connections.

When people and groups learn more, they develop a greater understanding of why people do what they do. This helps others learn from their experiences. As you research new topics and help others synthesize and connect these dots, take time to consider how your learning shapes the future each day.

Your motivation to help people keep learning will encourage the social circles around you to keep growing over time. As you and your teams accumulate more information and discover new patterns, you will likely be led in new directions. Be aware that people will look to you not only for new ideas but also as someone who is likely to have the most objective viewpoint about what to do next.

Developing other people is one of life's most important investments, and its effects last well beyond a lifetime. If you are motivated by developing other people, embrace it; engaging in this practice will enable you to have an outsized influence on the people you care about most. When you give people your undivided attention, it will help them to feel valued, learn, and make better decisions.

Groups will look to you when they want to be heard, grow, and have more engagement as a team. When you think about a specific person you want to invest in, try to notice how that person exhibits talents or potential in an area they have not explored. Describe what you see with specificity to get people excited about their work, and be sure to recognize small victories along the way.

You also have a unique opportunity to rally teams around common causes. The balance of talents within a team and the chemistry between people is often what determines their success or failure. Because you have a unique lens into the best way to develop each person, you are in an excellent position to help teams be more engaged and grow rapidly.

CONTRIBUTING TO TEAMS:

▶ When people can see and measure the way their work is improving other people's lives, they do better work and enjoy their jobs more. See if you can help bring more objectivity to group discussions about how your work is improving lives, and quantify this as much as possible.

▶ Be the voice of reason, results, and data when the teams around you are making decisions. While emotions and feelings matter, make sure you also come armed with facts so discussions maintain some objectivity about how to do the most meaningful work in the future.

▶ Identify one person who could benefit most by learning from your experiences and knowledge base. Dedicate at least an hour each week to the development and growth of this person.

▶ Think about how you intend to invest in the ongoing development of one specific person, and create a long-term plan for it today. There is likely no greater contribution you can make to someone's growth.

▶ Remember that while most of us likely do some meaningful work each day, we don't usually take the time to acknowledge or recognize these small victories. You can be the one who in almost any setting recognizes great work during a busy day.

▶ Teach people about the importance of identifying and building on natural talents. When you show other people not just how to uncover their strengths but also how to build on them, they can experience exponential growth.

CONTRIBUTING TO OTHERS' LIVES:

▶ In most working contexts, leaders greatly value people who bring them sources of information that lead to better organizational decisions. Identify one or two people who have the most respect for your work and think of a few new ideas or facts you could share with them today.

▶ People simply learn better in the context of a close friendship. Be there when someone needs you, whether they're a personal friend struggling with a health challenge or a colleague stressed about a work-related issue. Be a driving force for hope by bringing useful information and ideas to the surface.

▶ Continue to be a student of why people do what they do. Spend time every day observing the actions and reactions of your immediate social circles. See if you can identify a few patterns that could benefit from more awareness or investment of time.

▶ Make undivided attention your secret weapon in work and life. Be the one who does not have a smartphone out and who genuinely listens to every word when someone needs it. Simply doing this for 20 minutes is more of an investment in another person than you might realize.

▶ Identify a friend who is struggling to make an important decision, and help him or her work through their thought process as objectively and with as much information as possible. You can help them to make a better and more well-reasoned decision.

▶ Take a few minutes right now to see if you can identify hidden talents in two specific people — talents they likely have not seen in themselves. Watch to see if your instincts are correct; if they are, have a discussion with these two people, describing exactly what you saw and helping them see how they may be able to employ those talents more frequently in the future.

THE ENERGY TO BE YOUR BEST:

- ▶ The more you learn about the precursors to daily energy and good overall health, the more likely you are to act and change your own behaviors. Use your desire to know more: educate yourself about how the in-the-moment decisions you make can lead to more energy late in the day.
- ▶ There is so much disparate information about food, diet, and exercise out there today; see if you can be an oracle of clarity for the people around you when it comes to making healthy choices. While others are in the midst of fruit juice cleanses and the latest fad diet, be the person who brings some objectivity to the discussion about sustainable health.
- ▶ See if you can uncover a few new ways to get work done during your daily routine without sitting in a chair in a fixed position. At a minimum, find some way to ensure you are up and moving around at least a few times per hour.

▶ When you have developmental conversations with other people, try to do so while moving around. Whether you are outside or in an office, walk around instead of sitting in chairs. If you often have these conversations via audio, use a wireless headset to move around while you talk to create more energy.

▶ Help the people who look to you for guidance to identify some of their healthiest habits — the ones that give them energy during the day. Sometimes simply pointing this out leads to more learning and repetition of good habits.

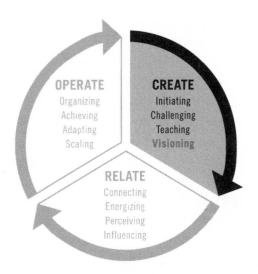

VISIONING

WHAT SHOULD WE DO NEXT?

*"The future belongs to those who believe
in the beauty of their dreams."*
—ELEANOR ROOSEVELT

People who are dreamers often need and get energy from time alone. They yearn for this time to ponder questions and generate new ideas. Even when they are in groups, they are often selective about what they say and prefer to listen or ask good questions of others.

In a world that talks a lot, it is likely your observations and ideas are not heard frequently enough. It is hard for your ideas to make a difference if they never enter the conversation. Be aware that people are far more likely to listen when you do speak up, as they know your thoughts may be more selective and influential. Using questions is another great way that introspective people can shape and influence group discussions.

People with more introspective talents are invaluable, especially given all the forces fighting for our attention today. When your team needs the opinions of someone who has done a lot of listening and thinking, speak up. Note all the detail, information, and ideas you have accumulated over time.

Almost every product, project, and organization starts with a vision that could lead to a better future. If you are motivated by visioning for new groups or initiatives, this is not just an essential element at the outset of the project; it's necessary to keep people moving toward a common vision each day. Having someone on a team who helps everyone to see a larger picture or imagine a better future can be one of the ultimate catalysts for growth, hope, and wellbeing.

Visioning is not just about lofty ideas. It is about deciding what ideas to invest in, bringing these ideas to life with words, leading a team forward, and keeping people focused on a common mission. Try to keep your focus on how these new efforts will improve a broader community, and be sure to help the people who look to you for vision see how their work will influence far wider audiences over time.

One of the challenges of having a lot of ideas is figuring out which ones deserve the most investment of time and financial resources. This is why it is important to test ideas early — to distinguish between those that can have the most positive influence on a broader community and others that may not resonate with a wider audience. In addition to being a big-picture idea person, see if you can become known for quickly sorting through ideas to identify those to double down on and others to cut loose.

CONTRIBUTING TO TEAMS:

▶ You likely need more time alone to generate ideas and meaningful thoughts, so reserve specific blocks of the day that will allow you to take this space.

▶ When you are in social circles, keep in mind that you don't need to talk anywhere near as much as the average person to derive meaning from the discussion, or to add value to it. Asking a few great questions and genuinely listening can be an even more important contribution to a group.

▶ When you do get time alone for thought, make sure you share at least some synthesis of your best ideas with another person. Your introspection likely generates substantive and thought-out ideas that others need to hear.

▶ Your natural tendency to focus on the longer term is a great asset for focusing on more meaningful work. Use this focus to help others pull their view up to a higher perspective on a regular basis.

▶ Keep in mind that others are listening to your words to see a bigger picture of what is possible. Continually test new ways of describing the vision you see to audiences and peer groups. Make note of the words, phrases, and stories that people say bring things to life best.

▶ At least once every two or three months, schedule a full day to step back and think about new ideas, products, and services that could be created from scratch instead of spending all your time on improvements to those already in existence. The people around you likely need someone to lead their thinking forward.

CONTRIBUTING TO OTHERS' LIVES:

▶ Remember that most great relationships are built one at a time. You're more likely to thrive in the context of regular one-on-one conversations versus a wide array of social interactions.

▶ Just like you need to take time for dedicated thought, block specific times or events for investing in learning more about the development of one other person through individual conversations.

▶ Help groups you are a part of understand the need to budget for time to look inward and be more reflective. When teams go through entire meetings or days where someone is always talking, no one has time to learn and absorb what's occurring.

▶ Most people are unlikely to find it as easy as you do to imagine a brighter future. See if you can spend time with two or three people in the next week who might need a little help in seeing what could be.

▶ In your next group or team discussion, keep bringing the conversation back to the broader community and how your efforts will improve lives in the end. Every group needs someone to bring this focus back as frequently as possible.

CREATE: Visioning

- Find one new way to help even wider audiences see or hear your vision for the future. Offer to teach or present to a larger group or author an article that can be shared with many.

THE ENERGY TO BE YOUR BEST:

- Look for ways to merge physical activity with time for thought. There is nothing better for creativity than time walking in nature, heading out for a run, or bike riding with a friend.
- Take a few minutes right now to take inventory of the things you have tried in the past that have benefited your diet, activity, and sleep practices. Then invest a little more time in the practices that have worked best based on your review.
- The more you learn and think, the more important it is to get at least seven to eight hours of sound sleep. This is what allows you to store all of the information you learned today and be a better learner tomorrow. Make a few small tweaks to the environment you sleep in to avoid disruptions in the middle of the night.
- Make sure your vision of the future includes finding new ways to get a little bit healthier every day. The teams

around you need you to be as energetic, creative, and inspirational as possible.

▶ Take time today to try to sketch a rough outline of how your physical health can be even better a year from today than it is now. Include specific strategies about how you plan to change the way you eat, move, and sleep.

▶ If you are feeling ambitious, see if you can map out structural plans to create healthier teams, organizations, and communities around you. There are a lot of structural and behavioral challenges that need to be addressed. And you have a unique lens for helping people imagine a brighter future.

CHAPTER EIGHT

RELATE

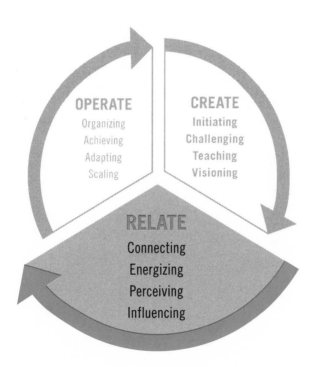

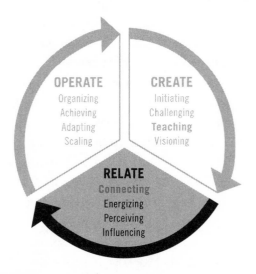

CONNECTING

HOW DO WE CONNECT PEOPLE TO OUR MISSION?

"You never really understand a person until you consider things from his point of view."

—HARPER LEE

People with a natural ability to make connections provide the spark for new conversations and can also enliven ones that are going quiet. They are often hubs for social networks, and they bring people together for gatherings, parties, and events. Connectors are energized by group interaction and add energy to conversations.

Connecting people can require a great deal of time and energy. Be aware that many people don't have your ability to initiate conversations or talk so freely and naturally. This means you may need to try even harder to bring them in by asking questions and pausing during conversation. If your goal is to add energy throughout the network, make these discussions as lively as possible for everyone.

There is no greater predictor of human wellbeing than the amount of social time we spend with one another. This is why having people with a natural talent for bringing others together and igniting conversation is essential to any group or organization. Take some time to observe how, when you're in action, the conversation moves with you and grows.

This also gives you a unique opportunity to stand up for what you believe in most deeply. If you are motivated by advocating for others, be their voice when they need it most. When friends or colleagues know they can count on you to help them be heard, they will trust you and look to you for guidance.

Advocating for products, services, teams, or initiatives you believe in can also be a powerful way to influence others.

You can be a great champion for people and causes. Watch for times when a person or project is in need of a boost. This is something you can deliver, often quickly.

There are countless topics people feel strongly about that they are not able or willing to publicly champion. While it is easier to see some of these examples in public and political life, they are far more common in classrooms, community groups, and work teams. If you are good at standing up for people and causes, look for opportunities to do it every day.

CONTRIBUTING TO TEAMS:

- ▶ You likely have a gift for bringing people together in groups. Think of a few new combinations of people you could bring together to achieve more as a team.
- ▶ Consider yourself one of the essential hubs for energy creation within your network. Map out your closest networks in your head or on paper. Determine which nodes need the most attention in order to thrive over the next six months.
- ▶ For friends, family, colleagues, and the communities around you to understand why your work is important, you need to articulate your key mission and purpose. You likely have a far better ability than most to put

what's most important into words. Help other people understand the meaning of your work.

▶ Start with what you, personally, believe in most deeply in life. Rooted in your belief and thinking is the ability to share and champion these core beliefs, and to educate the rest of the world about them.

▶ Consider the specific people you trust and care about most. Identify one or two people who can do extraordinary things. Invest an hour this month in talking with these people and thinking about how you can be a champion for their careers and lives.

▶ When it is time to share an important product, service, or mission with a wider audience, you can lead teams forward to create an even more successful launch. Use your ability to advocate to help potential customers see how these offerings will improve their wellbeing over time.

CONTRIBUTING TO OTHERS' LIVES:

▶ Starting a conversation may come naturally to you, but most people have trouble with it. When you are at group events, be on the lookout for circles that are struggling to get going. You can be the spark that turns that awkward dialogue into livelier conversation.

▶ Remember that some of the relationships you create between other people, even if you are no longer active in those relationships, can create a great deal of goodwill in the future. Make it your mission to create partnerships and teams with as much diversity of people and thought as possible.

▶ Spend more social time with the people you most enjoy being around. Even the most outgoing people do not spend enough hours per week socializing. Schedule a few more hours with the people who energize you most, starting today.

▶ When you are in meetings or group settings, be on the lookout for people who need to be heard. If you don't help them speak up, it's unlikely anyone else will.

▶ Because you are a champion for the people, they know they can count on you. When a friend who is more reserved brings something to you, pay careful attention, as people have learned that you will be an advocate when they need one most.

▶ You likely have a greater ability to detect both fairness and injustice than other people. Influence the future direction of your social circles by helping them improve the diversity of voices and opinions within them.

THE ENERGY TO BE YOUR BEST:

▶ Find ways to make your exercise routines as social as possible. The more you build them around your interactions with other people, the more likely you are to be active and participate.

▶ One of the challenges of being very active socially is that it involves a lot of dining out in groups. Find ways to get ahead of the endless temptations of bad choices by eating something healthy before you go to an event or setting rules for yourself about what to avoid.

▶ Try mixing socializing with physical activity, from going to the gym to long walks. See if this leads to even more positive and energizing interactions. If it does, encourage others to do the same and note how your example starts to change the dynamics throughout your networks.

▶ Identify friends and colleagues who set a great example in terms of valuing their own physical energy. Learn more about what they do. Then share with others what you see these people doing that the entire group can learn and benefit from.

▶ Consider some of the most effective ideas you have seen in terms of dietary changes, tips for better sleep, or workout routines. Be a champion for the ones that have worked and that you think others should learn more about in the future.

▶ As you study your normal working environment, identify a few ways in which you or others have built more activity into their daily routine. Be an advocate; help people see ways they can get work done without sitting for hours on end.

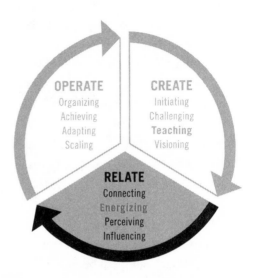

OPERATE
Organizing
Achieving
Adapting
Scaling

CREATE
Initiating
Challenging
Teaching
Visioning

RELATE
Connecting
Energizing
Perceiving
Influencing

ENERGIZING
HOW DO WE GET AND STAY CHARGED?

*"The best way to find yourself is to lose
yourself in the service of others."*
—MAHATMA GANDHI

People who energize us are more likely to bring joy to our daily routines and boost our wellbeing over the years. If you are motivated to inspire others, look for unique ways that your work can make people smile, laugh, and have fun. Use your tools, words, and stories to bring your ideas to life for friends, family, and others in your social circles.

Everyone is more creative, and able to achieve more in less time, when they are inspired. Boil things down to the basic elements to remind people why they do what they do. Bringing daily efforts back to this basic "why" can reenergize others' efforts. Notice how people can enjoy themselves more in the moment when you provide this inspiration.

Because most wellbeing is created in days and moments, you are in a remarkable position to substantively improve both the workplace engagement and daily wellbeing of people fortunate enough to be in your environment. Be the one who takes the responsibility for making a typical workday not only enjoyable but also fun. In the future, one of the primary reasons why people will continue to congregate in traditional office settings will be for the sake of building relationships and inspiring one another, and this is an area in which you can make an outsized contribution.

At the core of almost any group or organization of people is a mission or desire to serve others. If you are motivated by serving — loved ones, friends, colleagues, customers, community, or a higher power — this can be a remarkable way to exact a direct and meaningful influence through your work.

As we all move through our days, it is easy to take for granted the countless people who offer a little bit of their time to save our own time or make our days better. Yet these little moments where we interact with, take care of, comfort, or pick up the spirits of another person shape our daily well-being. When serving others, it is essential to see the impact of what you are doing in the moment, whether that influence is soothing a customer's aggravation through a phone call or getting a child to smile. These are substantive contributions we rarely take time to acknowledge.

See if you can not only respond to but also anticipate what the people you care about most may need. These efforts will serve broader communities over time and create a more sustainable environment for the next generation. It is this service — to a purpose beyond self — that keeps the entire network around you energized.

CONTRIBUTING TO TEAMS:

▶ Words can create an extraordinary amount of
  meaning in the world over time. Consider ways
  in which you can inspire others to laugh, smile, or

achieve extraordinary things using words people remember and find inspirational.

▶ For work to be sustainable day-in and day-out for decades, it simply has to be fun on a regular basis. See if you can notice how many people go from a negative or neutral state to smiling after their interactions with you. This can be a good barometer of how much positive energy you are infusing into a group each day.

▶ Help other people see how they can bring more joy and meaning to their work by sharing stories. For work to be meaningful, we need more stories about how a given person influences other people's lives in a practical way through their work. Teach people how bringing these stories to the forefront can lead to even better work in the future.

▶ You have an easier time than most people seeing how your work connects to a larger purpose. Use this talent to help the people around you see how their smaller daily efforts add up to something meaningful.

▶ Think about one thing you could do today to learn more about the specific people you serve through your work. Spend some time asking questions or interviewing a few of them. See if you can determine new ways to anticipate what they may need in the future.

▶ Step back and take inventory of how your work is creating more positive and sustainable energy for the future. As much as possible, remind yourself of the macro connections between your daily effort and all the people it serves.

CONTRIBUTING TO OTHERS' LIVES:

▶ Laughter and play are deeply underestimated elements of modern work environments. Think of two or three ways, right now, in which you could inspire people to simply have more fun during a typical workday.

▶ The people around you need inspiration to be more innovative and creative in their jobs. As you invest in the development of other people, see if you can help them spend more time on creative endeavors (if that fits their personality and work). There usually are ways to insert a bit of creativity into almost any task.

▶ Be the person who helps others by breaking abstract or complex topics down to their essential elements. You likely enjoy synthesizing and sharing information with wider groups. Doing this regularly can help ideas and projects to scale quickly.

▶ Try to focus more energy over the next year on how you can help entire teams to better serve the people who matter most. See if you can show others how you can collectively scale your missions to reach more people.

▶ You are likely better than most at comforting people when they need it. Identify two people in your circles of friends or colleagues who could use a little more attention in the next week. Simply spending time with them should boost their spirits and wellbeing.

▶ The more bridges you build between people and groups, the greater the audiences and communities you will be able to influence. Dedicate a little time every day to bringing people together and helping them to see the importance and influence of their daily work.

THE ENERGY TO BE YOUR BEST:

▶ Most people need inspiration in order to be more physically active throughout the day. Help people around you be creative about how they can craft a plan for building even a little bit of activity into their daily routine.

▶ Help people see how optimizing their physical energy levels is the key to having fun and achieving greater wellbeing each moment, each day. The more they prioritize sleep and the better their food choices in the morning, the more active they are likely to be throughout the day, and this creates upward spirals of better health and wellbeing.

▶ Today, make a list of the most common foods and meals that almost all experts agree are net positive for health and energy — foods like green leafy vegetables, nuts, legumes, and so on. Help others simplify and synthesize all the disparate information out there so eating well is that much easier for them.

▶ If you are better than most at juggling several tasks at once, try applying this to infusing movement into your workday — for example, find ways to talk or type while you are standing or walking.

▶ It's likely that your focus on serving other people in your community sometimes comes at a personal cost. Are you taking care of yourself to the degree you should? Understand that the people you hope to serve need you to take care of your own physical health first so they can count on you in a time of need.

▶ Think about a few health choices you could make that would offer you an immediate return. Would a brief morning run pick up your mood for the rest of the day? If you went to sleep 30 minutes earlier, would you have a bit more energy when you need it midday? See if you can draw a few direct connections between the choices you make and your energy that same day.

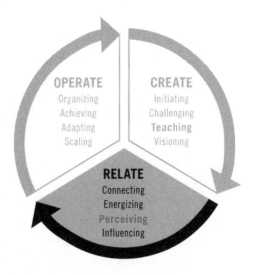

PERCEIVING
WHAT DOES EACH PERSON NEED?

"People will forget what you said, people will forget what you did, but people will never forget how you made them feel."
—MAYA ANGELOU

You have a gift for creating stronger bonds between people. You find commonality and consensus during conflict. You are likely a gifted listener and as a result can get along with almost anyone.

People probably bring their challenges and problems to you regularly, which can take a toll over time. When a friend or colleague is hurting, it can bring your mood down in parallel. Being aware of how this secondhand stress affects you can help you avoid trying to do too much in a concentrated period.

People with higher-than-average sensitivity have far more emotional awareness than others as they move through the day. They sometimes wear their emotions on their sleeve, and their mood fluctuates based on their interactions. This can be a huge asset for a team, as relationships with colleagues, customers, and friends are dependent on what occurs in these small exchanges throughout the day. Sensitive people are the ones who can help ensure your group is not scaring off or alienating the people you serve.

Being sensitive can also pose a real challenge. While those who know you well are likely more cautious about what they say in your presence, those who don't may use words that unintendedly offend you. Also be aware that while making the right choices is important, once you decide to move forward, regretting a choice you can't change often creates more stress than is necessary.

People with a more sensitive nature can keep us all grounded in human emotions. Almost all interactions in social groups are dependent on someone who can do a great job of gauging the emotional temperature in a room. Notice how your sensitivity can shape conversations, inform others, and be a sort of thermometer for the groups that surround your network.

You are the glue that holds groups, teams, and families together. These groups are likely more diverse and inclusive because of your efforts. Take time to note how your presence creates friendships, networks, and growth.

CONTRIBUTING TO TEAMS:

▶ Show others how the most meaningful work often occurs at the intersections between people.

▶ Use your natural ability to sense how people are feeling and to help ensure they see the bigger picture of why your group or team is doing what it is doing.

▶ Always be on the lookout for team members who do not feel included and need a little help to be brought into the fold of your group's greater mission.

▶ What makes moments most meaningful is the emotional imprint of interaction with another person. You have a greater ability to read into people's emotions and know what they are thinking, so help others to recognize moments that will have a lasting influence.

▶ You are more in tune with what is going on within a group or team on an emotional level, so help educate and inform others. Your influence can ensure that people don't rush to decisions without getting proper input from everyone involved.

▶ Your mood and stress levels are more likely to fluctuate with the ups and downs of a typical day. As this occurs, try to remember to not take it personally when people around you rush through tasks faster than you like; you are still all working toward a larger and more meaningful aim.

CONTRIBUTING TO OTHERS' LIVES:

▶ Continue to cultivate your reputation for being one of the best friends and listeners in your social circles. This is an increasingly rare quality, and it will hold even more value for others in the future.

▶ When two people are not getting along, be the one that brings them together for a direct conversation. Have confidence that doing this is almost always better than allowing ongoing silence between two people whose personal lives or work roles require that they have a relationship with one another.

▶ Because of your compassion, others' problems can drain your mental energy. Keep in mind that you do have a limited supply of relational energy.

▶ The people in your life likely know you have greater emotional awareness than most people. Keep an eye out for friends or colleagues you can tell are in need of a deeper conversation.

▶ Try to keep smaller stressors from derailing entire days. While your awareness can be a benefit at times, see if you can learn to manage your responses to common stressors to keep it from having a negative impact on your relationships.

▶ Understand that you may experience more fatigue from decision-making than your friends or family members. Help those around you understand that keeping things simple and less dramatic allows you to maintain a more constant and positive mood.

THE ENERGY TO BE YOUR BEST:

▶ Because of your sensitivity to the needs of others, it may be even more challenging for you to put your own physical health first than it is for others. Yet doing so is even more important for you, because it allows you to have the energy you need to be your best when serving others and taking care of those you love.

▶ Make physical activity a part of your social routine. Some of the best listening to friends and colleagues takes place amid a walking-and-talking session. Find ways to move more, even in small ways, when you are on the phone with people.

▶ As you are listening to friends and colleagues, try to hear and highlight places where they are setting a good example by making the right food choices, prioritizing sleep to be more effective, and so on. Help them build on their successes, and make an example of your own as well.

▶ The single best way to stay ahead of stressors and bad moods is to exercise regularly and get as much physical activity as possible. Try to build a little vigorous physical activity into every morning so you have a reserve against challenges throughout the day.

▶ Observe how your dietary choices, especially those you make early in the day, affect your energy levels in the mid-to-late afternoon. See if you can structure your earlier meals to be lighter; this will provide for better health and vitality later in the day.

▶ On days when you experience more stress than normal, remember that getting a good night of sleep gives you a full reset on the next day. Try to decompress in the hours before bedtime, avoiding electronic devices and bright lights.

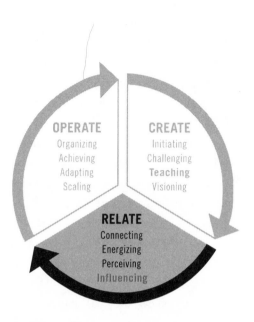

INFLUENCING

HOW CAN WE GROW OUR CLIENT BASE?

---

*"How wonderful it is that nobody need wait a single
 moment before starting to improve the world."*
—ANNE FRANK

The ability to be persistent and persuasive, and to influence others, is largely about sticking to what you deeply believe in and care about over time. While some people shift their beliefs, opinions, and efforts frequently, persistent people keep going even in the face of obstacles. Because they push through these obstacles, they often get far more done in a typical day than most.

Bringing people into new partnerships and relationships is how important people, ideas, products, and missions reach wider audiences. Be on a constant lookout for new ideas that need to be shared to improve lives. You can help a broader audience understand why they need to listen and pay attention.

Start by gathering the facts you need for your passion and credibility. Then try synthesizing, explaining, and sharing these concepts, first with circles of friends and then with more public audiences. Step back on occasion and think about the wider influence you are exerting and can exert in the future upon others. Building this legacy will help you continue influencing others every day.

Being persistent often requires defending your position and engaging in debate. This is a necessary and natural part of engaging in any group, but be aware that many others will shy away from confrontation and not hold a position as strongly as you will. And when others do hold a strong position, try to listen even more than you normally would so people know you are not overly dogmatic.

People who hold a deep belief and are willing to see it through are essential to the growth and formation of any group or organization. It is the people who persist who accomplish new things others did not think were possible. Even if your willingness to engage in debate creates conflict at times, take a moment to recognize the way your determination can carry a mission forward.

Consider some of the ideas that are shaping the industries and fields you care about most. Learn as much as you can about where these fields are headed. Then spend time practicing ways to bring these ideas to life with words to rally many more people. When you find ideas and topics worth investing in, spend several years, if not decades, teaching others about these topics.

CONTRIBUTING TO TEAMS:

▶ You are more likely to have a desire for working on big ideas and more substantial projects. In this age, where it is far easier to just respond to everything flying at you each day, this gives you a unique opportunity to help elevate people's perspectives every day — to encourage others to focus on the long term rather than the short term.

- Identify a subject in which you would like to be a world-class expert. Create a plan for learning, teaching, and scaling your knowledge around this topic.
- Many of the best ideas in life never have a chance to influence other people because there was no one to sell those ideas to the world — no one to convince people that they needed to listen to them. Find people, products, and services that others need to know about, and share them with the world.
- Creating works of substance that last often requires a great deal of persistence. When there are things that you believe in this deeply, keep investing in the knowledge you need to validate and support your point of view.
- You often get more done than other people do; use this tenacity to help others see how significantly certain ideas could scale and influence many lives over the next year alone.
- Even though you may prefer to stick with what you know and believe in, challenge yourself to try a few new things today. Have a conversation with someone you rarely spend time with. Try a new food. While it's great to enjoy what you know to be tested and true, allow moments when you let new experiences in.

CONTRIBUTING TO OTHERS' LIVES:

▶ While you're likely to recognize the value of sharing ideas you believe in with as many people as possible, keep in mind that it is also important to have a few people near you who are almost as passionate about the topic as you are and can help your work reach a larger audience.

▶ As you widen your social circles and share information, make sure you help people understand the objective value and credibility underlying your messages.

▶ A big part of your legacy will be the breadth and depth of the relationships you have created and the number of people who have become excited about what you believe in. As you look to the future, map out how this influence can be most effective.

▶ As a result of your persistence, friends likely know they can count on you during good times and tough times. Help friends see how your conviction in your beliefs is similar to your loyalty as a friend.

▶ Your enjoyment of debating topics when you are challenged and your tendency to stick to your beliefs can lead to conflict with friends and colleagues. Like you, some people enjoy this and learn from it. But be aware that other people can be frightened and recoil when they hear disagreement or debate.

▶ When a friend really needs to ensure that something will get done, they are likely to look to you for help. Use these experiences with friends to spend more time collaborating and learning about their perspectives on topics you care about deeply.

THE ENERGY TO BE YOUR BEST:

▶ There may be no larger influence you can have than helping people to make healthier choices and decisions in the moment. Use your passion for this to build a knowledge base of quick wins and ideas that will help people in your social network have more energy every day.

▶ Explain to people in very concrete ways how you have built more activity into your routine for the sake of managing your energy level throughout the workday. Give people realistic examples of how they can build more movement into their day, even if they are not interested in traditional exercise programs.

▶ Acknowledge that you are likely to have an outsized influence on other people's opinions and choices. This means people need to see you as a good role model in terms of how you prioritize your own health, your food choices, and the messages you send to people about putting their health first.

▶ Take a moment right now to think about the most effective fitness routines you have tried in the past. Create a schedule to repeat those activities again and again with consistency.

▶ Develop a system to track your activity, sleep, and diet. When you measure progress, you likely do better than other people at managing those elements over time. It does not have to be complicated. Just find a few shortcuts to holding yourself accountable.

▶ Because you are good at sticking with things past the point where others give up, continue to set more challenging goals around your food consumption, hours of sleep, and time spent moving around versus sitting throughout the day.

CHAPTER NINE

OPERATE

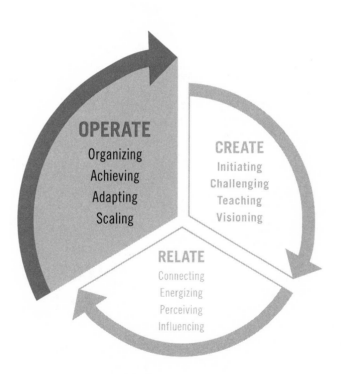

OPERATE
Organizing
Achieving
Adapting
Scaling

CREATE
Initiating
Challenging
Teaching
Visioning

RELATE
Connecting
Energizing
Perceiving
Influencing

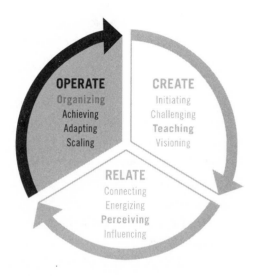

ORGANIZING

HOW DO WE MAKE THINGS RUN SMOOTHLY?

"Out of clutter, find simplicity. From discord, find harmony. In the middle of difficulty lies opportunity."
—ALBERT EINSTEIN

People with the unique ability to keep things organized ensure that expectations are met. They often prepare ahead, anticipating what will be next. If you are organized, people can likely count on you to be on time, if not early, for events.

A common challenge for people who are organized is that . . . not everyone else is. Be aware that your punctual nature and perfectionism can make things better for almost any group, but there will always be people who are late, disorganized, and so on. If you can help others anticipate and prepare, it may help you let go a bit and be in the moment at the time of the conversation or event.

Organizers keep all the people, places, and things in their networks moving in the right directions. They are often the fabric of the network itself, ensuring that work gets done at the right levels of quality. Take a moment every now and then to observe how much more smoothly things go on any given day because of the most organized people in your network, including you.

If you are motivated by structuring activities to make them safer and more reliable for others, embrace this quality; it can create a great deal of trust and confidence within your group. We all want to be prepared. But for this to occur, we need people we can count on when we need them most in every group and on every team.

This starts with finding common ground when groups are making their initial decisions. Testing processes to ensure they are reliable and identifying the causes of problems when things go awry also helps people feel more secure. This can apply to the dynamics of a team or the specifications of a product being manufactured. As you help secure things for others, take time to note how you are creating structures that will enable more rapid growth in the future.

CONTRIBUTING TO TEAMS:

▶ For any group or organization to have a wider influence, it needs a clear plan for execution; without a plan, it becomes an idea that never came to fruition. Help teams you are a part of break down the necessary steps to make a new product, service, or event meaningful for other people.

▶ You are more likely than most to think and plan ahead. This gives you a unique opportunity to anticipate what people will want in the future.

▶ Help groups and teams you are a part of understand the critical importance of meeting the expectations of the people you serve. You can be the voice of your customers and clients.

▶ Anything that is going to grow and influence large groups of people needs defined structure to enable that growth. Help your teams understand how the extra work you do now saves time in the future.

▶ An important step in almost any group or team initiative is ensuring that the appropriate people and parties are involved and there is general agreement on a path forward. Be the person who brings people and groups to a clear consensus about how to move forward.

▶ Remember that your efforts, even though they may take significant time, genuinely help people be more safe and secure. This is a contribution that may be hard to see in the moment but is the foundation for better experiences and greater wellbeing.

CONTRIBUTING TO OTHERS' LIVES:

▶ Think about your circles of friends and the groups you are a part of. It is likely that others look to you to plan and coordinate social events. Use this as an opportunity to structure more meaningful gatherings and experiences.

▶ Use your ability to stay organized to help friends and family stay on track. No matter how hard some people try, staying organized will not come as naturally to them, so they will rely on your lead.

▶ Your friends likely know they can count on you when they need it most. The next time a friend is in need, help them detail a concrete plan for getting back to a better place.

▶ Your efforts are likely helpful for finding consensus, maintaining peace, and avoiding conflict among groups. Identify one team at work that could benefit most from talking through a current challenge, and dedicate a few hours to this pursuit.

▶ Help your friends see that your often-cautionary tone is a product of how much you care about their safety and wellbeing. While some may perceive this as worry, make sure others understand that their long-term safety and security is the outcome you have in mind.

THE ENERGY TO BE YOUR BEST:

▶ Having a detailed and disciplined routine is one of the best ways to get and stay physically active. If you don't already have one today, create a plan for regular physical activity with built-in mechanisms for holding yourself accountable.

▶ Help your family members, friends, and colleagues see the benefits of keeping a more structured work schedule for the sake of sleep. Show people how the planning you do ensures that you get a solid seven-to-eight hours of sleep each night.

▶ Plan ahead for meals when you know options will be limited or you will be tempted to make a less healthy choice. Carry small, nutritious snacks with you when you're away from your home or office as well.

▶ When people experience regular stress and worry, it can override their mental energy and take a rapid physical toll. Think for a moment about a couple of the people in your social circles who seem to be under an unusual amount of stress. See if you can help them minimize the ways in which it is interfering with their routine.

▶ Help people see how small adjustments in their diet, sleep routine, and activity schedule can lead to noticeable and immediate changes in the amount of daily energy they have. Help someone connect the dots between a lighter lunch and less sleepiness mid-afternoon or an early-morning run and better ideas in a morning meeting.

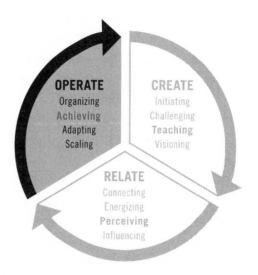

ACHIEVING

HOW CAN WE GET MORE DONE?

*"Always be a first-rate version of yourself, instead
of a second-rate version of somebody else."*
—JUDY GARLAND

People learn better through example, so they need leaders who are great role models. If modeling how to live, work, and do things well is one of your primary motivations, you probably are someone who influences others more so through actions than with words. When people see someone performing with excellence, they often want to learn and follow, even if it takes a little time for them to catch up.

Having someone in a group who can serve as an expert and focus on doing well in a specific area can help that team learn more rapidly. If being a role model for others motivates you, make sure you always keep your word and stay true to the ideals you are modeling. Remember, you are setting the trends for wider networks through your hard work and expertise.

One of the primary challenges in the modern workplace is that many leaders are poor role models themselves. While claiming they want everyone to make healthier choices, they are the ones who eat lousy foods, never work out, and email in the middle of the night. This creates a big opportunity for the next generation of workers, managers, and leaders in organizations. Those who can be successful at work while also focusing on maximizing their energy levels and overall well-being will be the new models for the future.

CONTRIBUTING TO TEAMS:

▶ One of the easiest ways to influence another person's behavior for the better is by simply setting a great example yourself. Take a couple of the topics you are most passionate about and think about how you can be an example of this behavior for others.

▶ Determine a way to (even subtly) observe how your modeling is shaping behavior around you over time. In some cases, it may take months or years for certain people to follow your lead.

▶ Pick one thing you think you can do at a level of perfection right now. Then determine how you can invest even more time and energy in this area of strength so you can be an even greater role model for others.

CONTRIBUTING TO OTHERS' LIVES:

▶ Your friends likely know you are incredibly true to your word and trust you unconditionally as a result. Therefore, it is critical to continue to keep your promises and deliver on these essentials of your closest relationships.

▶ Help others learn from your example by focusing on doing a few things very well instead of a lot of activities at a basic level of competency. Identify two people right now who could be experts in important areas if you were to help them to focus enough time and energy there.

▶ Because you are likely to work longer and harder than others, be sure to temper your expectations of friends and colleagues who do not want to run at the same pace.

THE ENERGY TO BE YOUR BEST:

▶ You are likely to be a trendsetter among your social circles. Because people are watching your actions, it is essential that your own daily routine showcases healthy food and activity choices, and valuing your sleep above almost all else.

▶ Become an expert on at least one specific topic related to leading healthier days. As people hear you talk about what you have learned and how you have changed your own habits, they will be inspired and follow your lead.

▶ When it comes to your activity or exercise routines, find one or two elements that really work, and ensure you practice them every day. One of the things needed most desperately in the modern workplace are examples of people who have built more movement into their daily schedule.

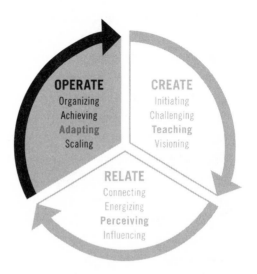

ADAPTING

HOW CAN WE ADAPT
QUICKLY TO CHANGES?

"Intelligence is the ability to adapt to change."
—STEPHEN HAWKING

When an environment is not fun, less gets done. By definition, natural improvisers help us all live a little. Life is created in the moment, and these small, often unscripted, interactions have an outsized influence on our days and lives. While many people get worked up over events that have not even happened yet, those who are spontaneous are better at adapting in the moment. They often work to the beat of their own priorities and expectations, which can be liberating.

By nature, improvisers live much less scripted lives. This often results in conflict with people or tasks that require more structure and sequence. Be aware that while many people need doses of spontaneity, they prefer more structure throughout a typical day. Help these people see how they can be more carefree and go with the flow at the right times.

Doing unexpected things is what makes life interesting. If not for the spontaneous moments, work and life would be routine and boring. Notice how your natural spontaneity livens moods in the midst of an ordinary day. You are also likely to be the person others know they can turn to for help when a situation does not play out according to expectations.

CONTRIBUTING TO TEAMS:

▶ Many of the most meaningful moments in life occur not in the context of grand events but when you least expect them. Your levity and spontaneity often allow these moments to occur naturally. Help others see how letting go of things, at least on occasion, can lead to a lot of fun and growth.

▶ Because you don't allow yourself to get as worked up over small things throughout the day, people will look to you to keep the spirits of a group high. Take a few moments to think about how you can help the groups around you add a bit more meaning to their daily routines.

▶ You are likely to set your own priorities and expectations in many cases. Help your friends and colleagues see how taking back a bit more personal control can give them the freedom and autonomy they need to be their best.

CONTRIBUTING TO OTHERS' LIVES:

▶ Most people realize that their more spontaneous friends provide them with a disproportionate amount of joy and wellbeing. Take a moment today to relish being the friend people look to when they need a major boost for their spirits. It is an important and substantive contribution.

▶ Be on the lookout for people who are creating undue stress for themselves by panicking about something that can easily be figured out at the last minute. You are likely to have a natural talent for making things happen when the time is right. Use this to illustrate how others don't need to waste precious moments stressing about things that will likely never happen.

▶ Keep in mind that other people may not be as carefree as you are. Consider your friends who need more structure in their lives, and try to meet them halfway when it comes to timing and planning.

THE ENERGY TO BE YOUR BEST:

▶ Use your knack for spontaneity to help groups take ad hoc breaks and outings. There is nothing better for a family, couple, or work team than an unplanned walk outdoors on a nice day.

▶ You are less likely to adhere to a strict schedule than most; this benefits you in many ways, but do find ways to at least budget for a full night of sleep. This will enable you to get a fresh start every day and have the energy you need to pick people up throughout the day.

▶ Look for ways to build healthy and unplanned breaks into your day. Find ways to move around every hour. Experiment with new ways to work while walking around. Test new ideas for healthy snacks and meals, and share them with others.

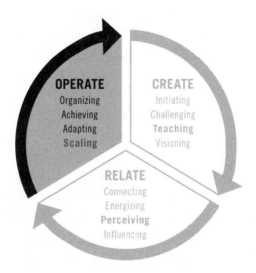

SCALING

HOW CAN WE REACH MORE PEOPLE?

"Without continual growth and progress, such words as improvement, achievement, and success have no meaning."
—BENJAMIN FRANKLIN

The ability to reach more and more people over time is what enables organizations to grow. If you are motivated by the thought of scaling up products, services, and efforts to reach more people, this can allow your efforts to have an exponential return. As consumers, we all want products that are more practical, applicable, and efficient. And we all want to maximize our time and effort. This is where the ability to scale can have a profound influence.

Scaling is often about finding the smartest ways to work and engineering things to be more efficient. Think about processes and technologies that could speed up the project you're working on or help your mission reach thousands more. Build bases of knowledge and financial resources dedicated to helping and reaching more people today. Make sure you take time to measure how many more people you reach as a product of your efforts.

As more and more routinized tasks become automated, people who can map out how to make things more efficient — not just for scale but also for time — will be increasingly essential. Anything you can do that saves other human beings time and effort will have deep value. See if you can be one of those people who help thousands of others spend more time on fun or enjoyable tasks through their work.

CONTRIBUTING TO TEAMS:

▶ Doing meaningful work requires focus. Your efforts to scale products and services can give other people time back for what matters most. Consider the people in your immediate circles right now, and determine one thing you could do so a few of them could have more time for meaningful work and conversations.

▶ Think about the way your work creates meaning for clients or customers. See if you can step into their shoes and, working backward from there, identify one improvement that would make things even more efficient for the people you serve.

▶ Technology often gets a bad rap for fragmenting attention, but it can also be a great way to make processes easier and scale concepts. See if you can find two or three ways in which technology could help someone you care about gain a greater insight into the meaning of their work.

CONTRIBUTING TO OTHERS' LIVES:

▶ See if you can help a few of your best friends find more efficient ways of doing things in their daily lives so they have additional time for thinking and socializing.

- ▶ Help the people around you more effectively prioritize the work they do so it has the maximum influence on the people your group serves.
- ▶ Remember that investing your time, energy, and financial resources in building closer relationships with family, friends, and colleagues is one of the best investments over time. These human connections are what most positively influence our daily wellbeing.

THE ENERGY TO BE YOUR BEST:

- ▶ Develop a plan to scale up your health. Think of all the things you could easily build into your daily routine that would give you little bursts of energy without taking up an undue amount of your time.
- ▶ Create scale and structure around your dietary choices so you have healthy defaults built into every day and are less likely to fall for tempting choices that will sap your energy.
- ▶ Help the people around you understand the necessity of prioritizing sound sleep first. Especially when work is busy, it is important for people to get enough rest so they can be their best all day, every day.

ONLINE RESOURCES

The Contribify.com website features a host of resources, articles, bonus chapters, and activities for individuals and teams. Visit the site today to explore the following resources:

- ▶ **Net Wellbeing:** A section with new research on how companies influence overall wellbeing and how you can measure it in your teams and organizations. Includes exclusive surveys describing how several large companies have positive and negative influences on our lives.
- ▶ **Building Teams with Cognitive Diversity:** A resource document for using Contribify for the development of any size team.
- ▶ **Management, Leadership, and the Workplace of the Future:** A special resource for developing people and getting ahead of the workplace of the future. Includes 15 predictions for the 2030 workplace.

- ▶ **Your Unique Purpose:** An overview of research that has been conducted on all of the things people do in various jobs.
- ▶ **Reflection and Portfolio Questions**
- ▶ **Worklife Wellbeing Questions, Tracking, and Assessment**
- ▶ **Amplifying Contribution:** An extended section on five key amplifiers for greater contribution.

REFERENCES

CHAPTER 1

1. Maddock, I. R., Moran, A., Maher, E. R., Teare, M. D., Norman, A., Payne, S. J., ... Evans, D. G. (1996). A genetic register for von Hippel-Lindau disease. *Journal of medical genetics*, *33*(2), 120-127. https://doi.org/10.1136/jmg.33.2.120

2. Turner, J. K., Hutchinson, A., & Wilson, C. (2018). Correlates of post-traumatic growth following childhood and adolescent cancer: A systematic review and meta-analysis. *Psycho-Oncology*, *27*(4), 1100-1109. https://doi.org/10.1002/pon.4577

3. Anders, G. (2013, September 4). Need a career tuneup? Gallup's Tom Rath has a quiz for you. Retrieved from https://www.forbes.com/sites/georgeanders/2013/09/04/how-gallup-hit-a-goldmine-with-strengthsfinder/#4c0fa083fb03

4. Rath, T. & Conchie, B. (2009). *Strengths based leadership: Great leaders, teams, and why people follow.* New York: Gallup Press.

5. StrengthsFinder 2.0 Gallup. (n.d). Retrieved February 11, 2019, from https://www.gallupstrengthscenter.com/home/en-us/strengthsfinder

6. Rath, T. (2007). *StrengthsFinder 2.0.* New York: Gallup Press.

7. Simon, M. D., & Dzhanova, Y. (2018, January 14). A guide to celebrate MLK Day across the country. Retrieved from https://www.nbcnews.com/news/nbcblk/martin-luther-king-jr-day-ways-celebrate-honor-mlk-s-n837656

8. CHANGE LIFE. (n.d.). It's what you can contribute. Retrieved from https://www.youtube.com/watch?v=WRYRBGX4lVM

9. Chancellor, J., Margolis, S., Jacobs Bao, K., & Lyubomirsky, S. (2018). Everyday prosociality in the workplace: The reinforcing benefits of giving, getting, and glimpsing. *Emotion, 18*(4), 507–517. https://doi.org/10.1037/emo0000321

10. Aaker, E. E. S., Jennifer. (2016, December 30). In 2017, pursue meaning instead of happiness. *The Cut.* Retrieved from https://www.thecut.com/2016/12/in-2017-pursue-meaning-instead-of-happiness.html

11. Christov-Moore, L., & Iacoboni, M. (2016). Self-other resonance, its control and prosocial inclinations: Brain–behavior relationships. *Human Brain Mapping, 37*(4), 1544–1558. https://doi.org/10.1002/hbm.23119

12. Aknin, L. B., Barrington-Leigh, C. P., Dunn, E. W., Helliwell, J. F., Burns, J., Biswas-Diener, R., … Norton, M. I. (2013). Prosocial spending and well-being: Cross-cultural evidence for a psychological universal. *Journal of Personality and Social Psychology, 104*(4), 635–652. https://doi.org/10.1037/a0031578

13. Fradera, A. (2017, July 4). Small acts of kindness at work benefit the giver, the receiver and the whole organisation. Retrieved from https://digest.bps.org.uk/2017/07/04/small-acts-of-kindness-at-work-benefit-the-giver-the-receiver-and-the-whole-organisation/

CHAPTER 2

14. Bryson, A., & MacKerron, G. (2017). Are you happy while you work? *The Economic Journal, 127*(599), 106–125. https://doi.org/10.1111/ecoj.12269

15. Pfeffer, J. (2018). *Dying for a paycheck: How modern management harms employee health and company performance—and what we can do about it.* New York, NY: HarperCollins.

16. Chandola, T., & Zhang, N. (2018). Re-employment, job quality, health and allostatic load biomarkers: prospective evidence from the UK Household Longitudinal Study. *International Journal of Epidemiology, 47*(1), 47–57. https://doi.org/10.1093/ije/dyx150

17. Surveys of 1,099 respondents conducted using Google consumer surveys. (n.d.). Google methodology available at http://services.google.com/fh/files/misc/white_paper_how_google_surveys_works.pdf

18. Hill, P. L., Turiano, N. A., Mroczek, D. K., & Burrow, A. L. (2016). The value of a purposeful life: Sense of purpose predicts greater income and net worth. *Journal of Research in Personality, 65*, 38–42. https://doi.org/10.1016/j.jrp.2016.07.003

19. Doing Good Is Good For You - 2013 Health and Volunteering Study - UnitedHealth Group. (n.d.). Retrieved from https://www.unitedhealthgroup.com/content/dam/UHG/PDF/2013/UNH-Health-Volunteering-Study.pdf

CHAPTER 3

20. Rath, T., & Harter, J. K. (2010). *Wellbeing: The five essential elements.* New York: Gallup Press

21. Kahneman, D., Krueger, A. B., Schkade, D. A., Schwarz, N., & Stone, A. A. (2004). A survey method for characterizing daily life experience: The day reconstruction method. *Science, 306*(5702), 1776-1780. https://doi.org/10.1126/science.1103572

22. Surveys of 1,034 respondents conducted using Google consumer surveys. (n.d.). Google methodology available at http://services. google.com/fh/files/misc/white_paper_how_google_surveys_ works.pdf

23. Missionday, (n.d.). Resource 4: Your Unique Purpose(s) [PDF File] Retrieved from https://contribify.com/wp-content/ uploads/2019/05/Contribify-Resources-4.pdf

24. Surveys of 1,016 respondents conducted using Google consumer surveys. (n.d.). Google methodology available at http://services. google.com/fh/files/misc/white_paper_how_google_surveys_ works.pdf

25. Surveys of 1,023 respondents conducted using Google consumer surveys. (n.d.). Google methodology available at http://services. google.com/fh/files/misc/white_paper_how_google_surveys_ works.pdf

26. Surveys of 1,503 respondents conducted using Google consumer surveys. (n.d.). Google methodology available at http://services. google.com/fh/files/misc/white_paper_how_google_surveys_ works.pdf

27. Surveys of 1,063 respondents conducted using Google consumer surveys. (n.d.). Google methodology available at http://services.google.com/fh/files/misc/white_paper_how_google_surveys_works.pdf

28. Harris, M. A., Brett, C. E., Johnson, W., & Deary, I. J. (2016). Personality stability from age 14 to age 77 years. *Psychology and Aging, 31*(8), 862–874. https://doi.org/10.1037/pag0000133

29. Spiegel, A. (2016, June 24). Invisibilia: Is your personality fixed, or can you change who you are? Retrieved from https://www.npr.org/sections/health-shots/2016/06/24/481859662/invisibilia-is-your-personality-fixed-or-can-you-change-who-you-are

CHAPTER 4

30. Longest ever personality study finds no correlation between measures taken at age 14 and age 77. (2017, February 7). Retrieved from https://digest.bps.org.uk/2017/02/07/longest-ever-personality-study-finds-no-correlation-between-measures-taken-at-age-14-and-age-77/

31. Howell, R. T., Ksendzova, M., Nestingen, E., Yerahian, C., & Iyer, R. (2017). Your personality on a good day: How trait and state personality predict daily well-being. *Journal of Research in Personality, 69,* 250–263. https://doi.org/10.1016/j.jrp.2016.08.001

32. Kaufman, S. B. (2016, August 5). Would you be happier with a different personality? The Atlantic. Retrieved from https://www.theatlantic.com/health/archive/2016/08/would-you-be-happier-with-a-different-personality/494720/

33. Wrzesniewski, A., Berg, J. M., & Dutton, J. E. (2010, June 1). Managing yourself: Turn the job you have into the job you want.

Harvard Business Review. Retrieved from https://hbr.org/2010/06/managing-yourself-turn-the-job-you-have-into-the-job-you-want

34. Cooks Make Tastier Food When They Can See Their Customers. (n.d.). Retrieved from https://hbr.org/2014/11/cooks-make-tastier-food-when-they-can-see-their-customers

35. Gino, F. (2017, March 6). To motivate employees, show them how they're helping customers. *Harvard Business Review.* Retrieved from https://hbr.org/2017/03/to-motivate-employees-show-them-how-theyre-helping-customers

36. Grant, A. M. (2008). The significance of task significance: Job performance effects, relational mechanisms, and boundary conditions. *Journal of Applied Psychology, 93*(1), 108–124. https://doi.org/10.1037/0021-9010.93.1.108

37. Grant, A. M., & Hofmann, D. A. (2011). Outsourcing inspiration: The performance effects of ideological messages from leaders and beneficiaries. *Organizational Behavior and Human Decision Processes, 116*(2), 173–187.https://doi.org/10.1016/j.obhdp.2011.06.005

38. Green, P., Gino, F., & Staats, B. R. (2017). *Seeking to belong: How the words of internal and external beneficiaries influence performance* (SSRN Scholarly Paper No. ID 2912271). Rochester, NY: Social Science Research Network. Retrieved from https://papers.ssrn.com/abstract=2912271

THE 12 CONTRIBUTIONS:

39. Mark Twain Quotes. (n.d.). Retrieved from https://www.brainyquote.com/quotes/mark_twain_118964

40. Indira Gandhi Quotes. (n.d.). Retrieved from https://www.brainy quote.com/quotes/indira_gandhi_163281

41. Nelson Mandela - Oxford Reference. (n.d.). Retrieved from http://www.oxfordreference.com/view/10.1093/ acref/ 9780191843730.001.0001/q-oro-ed5-00007046

42. Eleanor Roosevelt Quotes. (n.d.). Retrieved from https://www. brainyquote.com/quotes/eleanor_roosevelt_100940

43. *To Kill a Mockingbird* Chapter 3 Quotes Page 1. (n.d.). Retrieved from https://www.shmoop.com/to-kill-a-mockingbird/chapter-3-quotes.html

44. 12 Great Quotes From Gandhi On His Birthday. (n.d.). Retrieved from https://www.forbes.com/sites/ashoka/2012/10/02/12-great-quotes-from-gandhi-on-his-birthday/#74602aa633d8

45. Maya Angelou Quotes. (n.d.). Retrieved from https://www.brainy quote.com/quotes/maya_angelou_392897

46. Cannizzaro, A. (n.d.). Anne Frank - International Holocaust Remembrance Day. Retrieved from https://www.biography.com/news/anne-frank-international-holocaust-remembrance-day

47. Albert Einstein. (n.d.). Retrieved from https://www.buboquote.com/en/quote/4481-einstein-out-of-clutter-find-simplicity-from-discord-find-harmony-in-the-middle-of-difficulty-lies

48. Judy Garland Quotes. (n.d.). Retrieved from https://www.brainy quote.com/quotes/judy_garland_104276

49. Stephen Hawking Quotes. (n.d.). Retrieved from https://www. brainyquote.com/quotes/stephen_hawking_378304

50. Benjamin Franklin Quotes. (n.d.). Retrieved from https://www. brainyquote.com/quotes/benjamin_franklin_387287

CONTRIBUTIONS

My deepest gratitude to my dear friend and publisher, Pio Juszkiewicz, who has led the development and production of every book I have worked on over the last two decades. Pio is the ultimate book guru and partner on all of these projects.

While many people have contributed to the creation of this book, the following group of my closest advisors went above and beyond to make this book as clear and concise as possible: Ori Brafman, Chip Colbert, Kim Gladis, Steve Gladis, Margaret Greenberg, Senia Maymin, Andy Monnich, Ashley Rath, Connie Rath, and Peter Sims.

Nick Alter, Aubrey Berkowitz, and team led the development of the Contribify.com website, inventory, and profile, which we hope will grow and expand over time.

We continue to have some of the best design, editing, and production partners in the business, including Domini Dragoone, Krissa Lagos, Emily Loose, Paul Petters, and Salman Sarwar.

To all of the other people who contributed to the ideas, research, and development of this book, my team and I offer our deepest gratitude.